TRANSCONTINENTAL PEDESTRIANS

Canada's First Cross-Country Walk (1906)

George Edward Hart

Introduction by

Jonathan Vance

D0786157

Fitzhenry and Whiteside Limited
195 Allstate Parkway
Markham, Ontario L3R 4T8

In the United States:
311 Washington Street,
Brighton, Massachusetts 02135
www.fitzhenry.ca   godwit@fitzhenry.ca

Fitzhenry & Whiteside acknowledges with thanks the Canada Council for the Arts, and the
Ontario Arts Council for their support of our publishing program. We acknowledge the finan-
cial support of the Government of Canada through the Book Publishing Industry
Development Program (BPIDP) for our publishing activities.

ONTARIO ARTS COUNCIL
CONSEIL DES ARTS DE L'ONTARIO

Canada Council   Conseil des Arts
for the Arts   du Canada

Library and Archives Canada Cataloguing in Publication

Hart, George E
Transcontinental pedestrians: George E. Hart.
Canada's First Cross-Country Walk (1906)
ISBN 1-55041-345-7
1. Gillis, John High. 2. Jackman, Charles. 3. Walking—Canada.
4. Canada—Description and travel. 5. Cape Breton Island (N.S.)—Biography.
I. Title.
FC74.H355 2006   917.104'56   C2005-906616-4

United States Cataloguing-in-Publication Data
Hart, George E.
Transcontinental pedestrians : Canada's First Cross-Country Walk (1906)
/ George E. Hart ; introduction by Jonathan Vance.
[256] p. ; photos., maps ; cm.
Summary: In the winter of 1906, three young, fit men from Cape Breton set out from
North Sydney to walk across the continent and return within a year.
ISBN: 1-55041-345-7
1. Walking—Canada. 2. Canada--Description and travel. 3. Gillis, John Hugh.
4. Jackman, Charles. I. Vance, Jonathan. II. Title.
917.104/56 dc22   FC74.H378 2006

Cover & interior design by Karen Thomas, Intuitive Design International Ltd.
Cover photo by P.N. Crandell, Moncton, 1906,
courtesy of Beaton Institute, Cape Breton University, no. 83-661-13962
Maps by Kerry Designs
Printed and bound in Canada

1 3 5 7 9 10 8 6 4 2

To my wife during sixty-three years,
Jean Jackman, who died 26 August 2005.
Thoughtful, fun-loving and artistic,
it was her way always to find a connection to others.

Contents

Foreword & Acknowledgements

A hundred-year-old diary, bound in dark red morocco leather and as small as a woman's hand, came into my possession the summer before last. Charles Henry Jackman, young business man and retired lacrosse player, had recorded his daily experience of a last testing adventure – a trek on foot from one side of the continent to the other. He had had his diary stamped by an agent of the Canadian Pacific Railway at each station he passed. He had also snapped two hundred and fifty photographs, of which only fifty-seven have survived. In his later years he told me, his son-in-law, stories about that dramatic episode in his young life. My son Jonathan talked with Michael Davis, a Fitzhenry & Whiteside editor, and as a result the firm showed an interest in publishing a commemorative book. *Transcontinental Pedestrians* is the result.

Although a good foundation for this book, the diary was not enough. In fact, it created many blanks that required extensive research to fill: for example, it mentioned a friend and fellow tramper, Gillis, never giving his first name. Only the newspapers of a hundred years ago have enabled the rediscovery of much of this adventure.

Once establishing that there were four characters in the venture, the next step was to get in touch with their families. False trails sometimes led to wasted time and money. Advertisements in newspapers in Sydney, Halifax, Pictou and New Glasgow offering a reward for information resulted in contact with several members of the Gillis family and eventually with the right Cumming family.

Unfortunately, letters and most other records about the 1906 adventure have not survived with those families. Gillis had his own camera with him and had the signatures of mayors or clerks of towns he passed through. He also had letters from friends and relatives and newspaper clippings. Family memory seems to indicate that after his death a sister took all his memorabilia to her home in Dartmouth and that those historic treasures burned in a house fire.

The recollections of various family members have been most helpful. George Cumming's mementos preserved in two little black boxes were thrown out many years after his death. Birth, marriage, census and hospital records and obituaries have helped to fill in the pasts of those pioneer characters and events. Again, the recollections of a granddaughter have been invaluable.

Given the wide geography of the adventure, the making of the book became a team effort. Margaret Gillis, of Halifax, diligently searched newspaper items and also presented information about the Highland origins of this Gillis family. Norman Gillis, of South West Margaree, told about the early years of the settlement. Reginald Jobe, of North Sydney, provided photographs of trophies. Other members of the Gillis family helped: Carol Capstick and Barbara MacNeil, of North Sydney, and Sandra Vallar, of Sydney.

Responding to an advertisement, Mr. Justice Clyde F. MacDonald, a Cumming cousin of New Glasgow, brought new hope late in the search for the family origin and later career of George W. Cumming by sending his book *More Notable Pictonians* and George's obituary. Judy Maliff, of LaSalle, Quebec, George's granddaughter, provided a photograph and interesting accounts of George's later years.

My own family contributed greatly to the content of the last chapter, my wife Jean especially and Charles, of London, England, Gwendolyn Brown, of Mississauga, Deborah Elder, of Guelph, Alan Hart, of Vancouver and Seattle, Jonathan Hart, of Edmonton, and Jennifer Hart, of Toronto. Alan spent much time finding many important items in the newspapers of Vancouver and Kamloops and both he and Jonathan made helpful suggestions. Charles's childhood memories of his grandmother have added to the picture.

Independent researchers have contributed much to the knowledge base of this book: Kathleen Bain for search of Vancouver Directories; James P. Barnaby, of Halifax, on the career of Henry Martin Bradford; Madeleine Best, of Stockport, Manchester, England, for scanning newspapers for lacrosse sports items relating to Charles Jackman; Marlene Chisholm, C.G.(C), of New Glasgow, most especially, for intelligent and meticulous search for the family and career of John McDonald and for scanning many issues of the *Sydney Daily Post* for items about Gillis's walk; Mildred Howard, C.G.(C), of Sydney, for genealogical work; Ruth Z. Lewis, C.G., of Lansing, for search of Michigan newspapers; Leila Muldrew for scanning Victoria newspapers from October 1906; Sheila Norton, C.G.(C), Victoria, for search of documents pertaining to the Tranquille Sanatorium.

Various institutions have provided gratefully received service and information: Archives nationales du Québec; Beaton Institute, University of Cape Breton; British Columbia Archives; British Columbia Genealogical Society; Canadian Pacific Railway Archives; Canadian Railroad Historical Association; Census of Canada; Chicago Public Library; Michigan City Public Library; National Library of Canada; Natural Resources Canada; North York Public Library; Pictou County Genealogy and Heritage Society; Public Archives of Nova Scotia; Quebec Family Historic Society; Revelstoke Museum and Archives; St. Francis Xavier University Archives; St. Joseph's Library of South Bend, Indiana; Toronto Reference Library; Trent University Archives; Vancouver Police Museum.

The editors gave much of their knowledge and experience to the shape and texture of this book. Michael Davis has managed the project in a friendly and effective way and has been quick to foresee and analyze story-line issues. Penny Hozy, as a novelist and editor, suggested the very shape of the book and has been most sensitive in smoothing out the narrative and at the same time respecting the author's voice. Richard Dionne provided the final touches, supervising the design and visual components of the book. Working with the editors of Fitzhenry & Whiteside has been a creative pleasure.

In 2004 the author nominated John Hugh Gillis for induction into the British Columbia Sports Hall of Fame and the Nova Scotia Sports Hall of Fame. The BC Hall inducted Jack Gillis May 10, 2006, as a great pioneer, all-round athlete.

JOHN HUGH GILLIS

Turn-of-the-century athlete died before he could attend Olympics

An Upper Margaree man whose athletic ability was Olympian in its potential, died before he could measure his ability against the best in the world.

John Hugh Gillis, born in

A nephew of Margaree Bard Malcolm H. Gillis, he walked from North Sydney to Vancouver. It took him three months. In Vancouver, he joined the police force and was a desk sergeant. His

Introduction by Jonathan Vance

Nineteen hundred and six doesn't usually rank as a banner year in Canadian history. No wars started or ended, there were only two general elections, in British Columbia and Nova Scotia, and there were no great natural disasters to horrify the readers of Canada's daily newspapers. Granted, cigar-box manufacturer Adam Beck did establish the Ontario Hydro-Electric Power Commission, bringing to Canada the age of public electricity, and John Griffins opened the first Canadian string of cinemas. Tommy Burns (who was raised not far from Beck, although 'on the other side of the tracks') won the world heavyweight boxing title and Bill Sherring of Hamilton won the Olympic marathon, both Canadian firsts. But it was also the year that four young men took part in what can only be called an odyssey: a journey across the continent on foot. Their epic trek made for the kind of news story that was a welcome diversion for the six million Canadians who were just getting on with the business of making a living.

In Gillis's home turf of Cape Breton Island, despite the fact that Sydney was soon to become an industrial powerhouse, much of the region appeared to be frozen in an earlier time. The displaced Highlanders still tilled the land as their ancestors had for generations, and many of them preferred to speak Gaelic rather than English, the language of the men who had forced them from their Scottish homes. It was the same elsewhere in the Maritimes, though Halifax and Saint John carried on a friendly (and sometimes not so friendly) rivalry over which city represented the pinnacle of modern commercial development. Prince Edward Island remained in splendid isolation from the rest of Canada; the ice boats that crossed between the island and the mainland in the winter really didn't provide the "continuous communication" that had been promised in the terms under which the colony agreed to join the Dominion.

Montreal still laid claim to being the largest city in the Dominion (with over 140,000 people), as well as the centre of business and commerce, but like all of Canada's new cities, it was a place of extremes. The opulent mansions of the Golden Mile and the stately head offices along St. James Street contrasted sharply with the other Montreal: the slums hugging the Lachine canal, clustering around the rail yards in the east end, and fringing the port. There, grinding poverty led to scenes of unimaginable suffering – one contemporary magazine carried an illustration of two children who had frozen to death in their hovel, for the family couldn't afford coal or wood for the stove.

It was the same scene of misery amidst plenty in Hamilton, Toronto, Brantford, Trois-Rivières, Windsor, London – any of the cities in central Canada that were rapidly industrializing. Ottawa was a little different. The rough-and-tumble lumber town that Queen Victoria had selected as the capital of the Canadas was settling in as the political centre of the nation, but even so the grand Parliament Building, completed in 1866 and declared to be one of the finest public buildings in the world, looked across the Ottawa River at the smoking factories and grim shantytowns of Hull.

Still, the social and political elites worked hard to sell the era as an age of optimism and progress. Nation-building was the order of the day – "The nineteenth century was the century of the United States," Laurier told voters during the 1904 election campaign. "I think that we can claim that it is Canada that shall fill the twentieth century" – and the Knight of the White Plume set about pushing back the boundaries of settlement, to make Canada the world power that he believed it could be. In 1889, Sir John A. Macdonald had shifted Ontario's border northwards by hundreds of miles; in 1898, Laurier did the same for Quebec. The Yukon District had been created in 1895; three years later, Laurier gave it territorial status. Perhaps most importantly, his government created the provinces of Saskatchewan and Alberta in 1905 – no longer would Manitoba be the focal point of the west.

And it was in the west that the Laurier boom was most visible. The government's campaign to fill the western plains with "stalwart peasants in sheep-skin coats," as Minister of the Interior Sir Clifford Sifton called them, had paid off in spades, turning the three prairie provinces into the fastest growing region in Canada. From just under 100,000 in 1881, the population had exploded to over 800,000 in 1906, and the growth of the urban west was even more staggering. Every major city on the prairies – Winnipeg, Regina, Calgary, Edmonton – more than doubled in population between 1901 and 1906; Saskatoon had thirty times more people in 1906 than it had five years earlier.

Much of this growth was based on the wheat economy, something that had scarcely existed when the walkers were born. The first exports of wheat from the prairies to Great Britain hadn't left Manitoba until 1877, but by 1906 millions of bushels were handled by the grain exchange in Winnipeg every year. The prairie west was dotted with grain elevators – there had been only a handful in 1885, but by 1906 there were over a thousand – and overlaid with spider webs of railways. Although the CPR still ruled the roost, the Canadian Northern and the Grand Trunk Pacific were expanding dramatically, opening up new areas to agriculture and causing towns to spring from the prairie earth in their wake. Between 1881 and 1911, railway mileage more than quadrupled, with passenger traffic nudging towards forty million people a year in the same period. And all along the lines were the stations, junction houses, switching huts, and repair depots that the pedestrians would come to rely on for food and shelter.

Over the Rockies, two gold rushes had fuelled British Columbia's economy in the 1850s and 1860s, then died out, leaving the province to endure a series of boom-and-bust cycles before hard-rock and coal mining arrived. Despite an influx of immigrants from Asia, the province was still very British – the Royal Navy maintained a garrison at Esquimalt until 1905 – and there was a strong rivalry between Victoria and Vancouver. Victoria was the site of its capital, but Vancouver's economic importance was on the rise. It was a contest that dragged on for years, and many people in the province still looked back fondly on the days when Vancouver Island and British Columbia were separate colonies.

In short, the twentieth century had dawned, and the four walkers found that their journey took them through a vastly different country than the one their parents had known. In the early twenty-first century, we like to imagine that we inhabit a world of dizzying change; it gives us, rightly or wrongly, a comfortable assurance of our own adaptability. But the changes that we have seen over the last twenty years are nothing compared to what the transcontinental pedestrians had witnessed, even before they set out from North Sydney on a cold January morning. Cumming, Gillis, and McDonald (Jackman was the only immigrant among them) were born into a land of horse-drawn buggies and water power, of frontiers yet to be opened. The post was the only reliable means of communication, and the most isolated homesteaders could go for days before learning that the government had fallen or the prime minister had died. For the majority of Canadians, cities were the exception rather than the rule, mechanization was something that most folk just talked about, and people's lives were governed by the rhythms of the day and the season rather than the clock.

By 1906, all that had changed. Canada was still predominantly rural, at least in a statistical sense, but the growing cities were acting like magnets, drawing immigrants (like Charles Jackman) from abroad and from the country districts alike. They were now places of electric streetcars and lights, thick canopies of telephone, telegraph, and electric wires hanging over the sidewalks, automobiles that made horse and pedestrian equally nervous, and moving-picture palaces with blinking marquees. What's more, these newfangled contraptions were starting to move out of urban Canada. Farmers were establishing telephone cooperatives and figuring out ways to bring electricity to their hamlets. They were even starting to buy cars.

If it was the age of optimism, it was also the age of invention. The gramophone had been invented in 1887, the diesel engine in 1898, and neon light in 1902. Marconi sent the first wireless message across the Atlantic in 1901, and the Wright brothers flew the first airplane in 1903. Everything from the machine gun and barbed wire to corn flakes and the tea bag had been invented in those decades. It would be difficult to find another era in which so many discoveries were made in so short a time. The world of these four men had been re-shaped in the few years it took them to reach adulthood.

And yet they chose to make their crossing of the continent by the oldest form of transportation, on foot. Sir John A. Macdonald, the prime minister whose dream built the railway they walked along, would probably have appreciated the determination of fellow three Scots (and one Englishman) in a cause

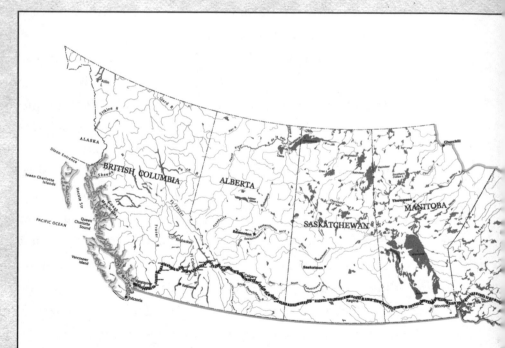

Gillis and Cumming had a map of the route. They would follow the Intercolonial Railway to Saint John, the Canadian Pacific to Montreal, the Grand Trunk to Chicago and the Union Pacific to San Francisco.

that had just enough madness in it to make it interesting. And he would have approved of the symbolism of walking from one side of the continent to the other along the iron rails he fought so hard to build.

Were they trying to come to terms with their changing world, these young men who had been born into a traditional, rural society but who had embraced the modernism of city life? Was it a reflection of the popularity at the time of long-distance runs and walks as spectator sports? Was it for the money, a not inconsiderable sum in those days? It could have been any of these, or perhaps it was none of them – perhaps it was just something they wanted to do.

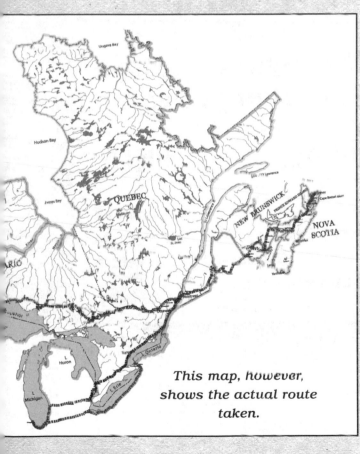

This map, however, shows the actual route taken.

EDITOR'S NOTE:

Imperial measurements are used throughout this book.

To convert:

1 mile = 1.6093 kilometres

1 yard = 0.9144 metres

1 inch = 2.54 centimetres

1 acre = 0.4047 hectares

1 pound = 0.4536 kilograms

DAILY POST. MORNING EDITION

EY, C. B. MONDAY, JANUARY 29, 1906.   PRICE TWO CENTS

ALLEGED GRAFT IN RECENT DEAL

Charge Made by Halifax Alderman.

TWO TENDERS

He Says that C——
now a
ton, has
as the
Island
ince of
r, holds
militia,
South
a wing
llegiate
sent in

(Special Despa——)
HALIFAX, Jan.——
has been opposing th——
fire engine offered b——
company in London——
with a statement t——
mittee meeting, that——
ders from the cham——
dred dollars——
addressed to the m——
that only one of th——
higher, while the c——
copy of the tender——
He would not give it——
however, obtained it——
Saturday, went to th——
and captured the ten——

THE KING OF SPAIN AND HIS BRIDE

HIS OFT REPEATED

Rumors That Attempt——
to Prevent the——
William Seek L——
in December.

(Special Despa——)
BIARRITZ, Ja——
Alfonso did not——
Sanatberdian, this——
morning, after th——
who is stopping——
he started for——
m. It was ver——
sety early in th——
inside. The P——
Princess Ena, the——
weather having——
on an automobil——
here again——
thing King Alf——
at San Sebastian——
eive Princess——
there on Sunday——
Among other——
German intrigue——
ment of the Kin——
is said that some——
were compelled to——
front entering int——
alleging that the——
It is even said——
liam instructed h——
to influence aga——

H.M.S. DOMINION HAS SAILED FOR PORTLAND.

HER DESTINATION WAS AT FIRST KEPT SECRET.

There was Less Than a Foot of Water Under Her Bow as she lay at the Dockyard Pier—In Turning in the Harbor She Showed Good Steering

STEAMER AMETHYST HAS REACHED NORTH SYDNEY

MADE FAST RUN BETWEEN CAPES SPEAR AND RACE.

Property at Northwest Arm Contains Valuable Deposits of Fireclay—Sudden Death—Goods Auctioned—Accid——

LIQUOR DESTROYED.

Campaign of the Temperance People of McKay's Corner Against Liquor.

(Staff Correspondence.)
GLACE BAY, Jan. 28—Yesterday the Grand liquor to the value of $40 or $50 was destroyed in front of the town hall.
Some months ago the people of McKay's Corner took a decided stand against liquor traffic in that section of the town. They decided to close up every rumshop in the place. The set about their work quietly but effectively, with the result that today the district is completely rid of saloons.
All those engaged in the liquor business, with the exception of one, quietly closed up as soon as they realized the

death occurred quite recently.
Messrs. Kawaja Bros. have removed their business to the premises recently occupied by Mr. John Nader on Commercial St.
D. J. Corbett, of Kirk-Whitman Tailoring Co., left this morning on a two weeks' vacation to his home in Prince Edward Island.
Arrangements for the funeral of the late Benjamin Langille will not be made until his sons, William and Daniel, arrive home Monday night.
The funeral of the infant daughter of Capt. Blackmore will take place tomorrow to Lakeside Cemetery.

SANTO DOMINGO'S DEBT.

United States Commission Places the Total at $40,269, 404.83.

(Associated Press Despatch.)
NEW YORK, N. Y., Jan. 28—Washington advices to the Herald say that

WILL WALK TO SAN FRANCISCO

North Sydney Boys Will Attempt Feat.

TRIP 8,000 MILES

Dollars J. H. Gillis a——
mings Will Endeavor t——
Golden Gate and Retu——
year.

of $600 two North S——
Messrs. J. H. Gillis an——
agreed to tramp to S——
ack, a distance of abo——
journey to be accom——
The terms of the——
that the men shall se——
ney without a cent——
will be given a char——
ties which they must v——
ute. At each of th——
obtain a written sta——
mayor or other prom——
prove their visit. I——
known sport across——
with several other m——
necessary inducem——
make the trip. The r——
ll start at 7 a. m.——
from the Terminus,——
the boys intend ke——
track as far as Po——
ney will branch off on——

a native of North S——
bin athletic career——
ears has become famil——
oughout the lower pr——
h who could make——
ort. His particular——
work. At present——
pionship of Cape Bre——
above five miles. Wh——
F. X. College at A——
many medals which h——
city as a good one w——
Mr. Gillis and t——
stocking feet, is of——
y physique, and if th——
t this end of the co——
depended on to fin——
inside the required ti——

a native of New G——
up to date he has ne——
startling effect in——
he nevertheless ha——
native grit, which a——
finish of the journe——
torms have undertake——
as to make the dist——
limit they must trav——
les a day.——
evening the plucky a——
endered a banquet b——
friends at the Qu——
following morning th——
dust of Cape Breton——
turn their faces in th——
Golden Gate.——
er gives the credit of——
endurance test. He wi——
couple of other sports across the——
put up the money, which is to be p——
in one of the local banks until——
period of twelve months has passed.——
men will be sent away on Wednes——
morning at 7 a. m. by Mr. Parker.——

PACIFICATION AT THE FINAL STAGE

TWO HUNDRED AND FIFTY RE-LUTIONISTS SHOT.

Several Thousands Under A——
5,000 Rifles Captured—M——
lutionists are Entrapped in——
of 10,000 Troops.—Leaders Wi——
Shot.

(Associated Press Despatch.)

DAILY POST.

WILL WALK TO SAN FRANCISCO.

North Sydney Boys Will Attempt Feat.

ROUND TRIP 8,000 MILES.

For Six Hundred Dollars J. H. Gillis and George Cummings Will Endeavor to Reach the Golden Gate and Return Within one year.

LIVES OF 800 PEOPLE IN DANGER FROM FIRE.

SERIOUS CONFLAGRATION IN BEL-LEVUE HOTEL——

The Sixan Which Woke the Laundry——
Kathleen, the Awaken——
'Any of the Pitians Firemen——
Responded with Heavy Wheel——
He Lives Lost.

(Associated Press Despatch.)
NEW YORK, Jan.——Eight hundred patients in Bellevue Hospital were endangered by a fire in the laundry build——

Starting Out

The crisp morning of Wednesday, January 31, 1906, a large crowd gathered at an unusually early hour in the station house of the Intercolonial Railway at Commercial Street in North Sydney, Cape Breton. It was fifteen minutes to seven. Mayor Hackett was there. So were the parish priest, the president of St. Joseph's Association, the head of the League of the Cross, at least one of the six betting sportsmen and, of course, reporters from *The Sydney Record* and the *Sydney Daily Post*. Family members and friends attended to see off the two young men on whom all eyes were focused. The two had made a strange bet, and they were going far. Donald Parker, a well known sport and man of business, had promoted the event that brought the intrepid travellers together on this chilly morning. Those who cared had happy and sad-anxious feelings about the two young men, whom they likened to old-time seamen sailing halfway around the world and, God willing, coming home to port many months later.

North Sydney was a busy town. It ranked third among the great ports of Canada, shipping coal and steel and providing a ferry connection with Newfoundland. It had a polyglot population but the Highland Scots who came in the 1820s brought with them a distinctive culture of Gaelic music and dancing, and the athletic tradition of the Highland Games. By 1840, twenty thousand Scots were settled in Cape Breton. In the late 1800s Gaelic was the third most common European language in Canada. That heritage created in North Sydney the St. Joseph's Association for the physical, mental and moral development of young men of the parish. Its three-storey Empire Hall provided a reading room, library, bowling alley, gymnasium, and space for concerts and dances. Here the young athletes gathered as members of the League of the Cross.

In that library they most likely read Stephen Powers' *Afoot and Alone*, republished by the Columbian Book Company in 1884.[1] A Civil War reporter, Powers left Raleigh, North Carolina, on January 1, 1868, and made his way slowly, on foot, on main roads and railroads, noting the society through which he passed, until, after 3,556 miles, he reached San Francisco early in November. Perhaps the North Sydney lads also read *A Tramp Across the Continent*, published in 1903 by Charles Scribners Sons,[2] wherein Charles Lummis, a dashing young journalist, described his walk of 3,500 miles from Cincinnati on September 12, 1884, to Los Angeles on February 1, 1885. Maybe one, or both, of those books inspired them to talk about such feats of endurance with their sportsmen friends, many of whom may have been ready to push talk into action for a monetary incentive?

Loading the British Mails at North Sydney

One night at the Hall, an argument arose among the young athletes as to whether noted long-distance runner John Hugh Gillis had what it took to walk to San Francisco and back. George W. Cumming, storyteller and singer, thought he did and volunteered to accompany John Hugh on such a trek. Three newspapermen and three prominent sportsmen of North Sydney (a real betting town, complete with racetrack) and Sydney, headed by Don Parker, John Hugh's brother-in-law, put forth a plan for an ultimate test of endurance and enterprise. They offered the two men a total of $600 each, if they would leave North Sydney with no money in their pockets, walk to San Francisco and back within a year, returning with $200 each in their wallets. (The prize money was to be held on deposit in the Royal Bank from day one of the trek.) Six hundred dollars was a big inducement in those times. A skilled carpenter earned about $600 per year; a first-class male teacher a little less than that; hourly workers up to $375 per annum; and white collar workers up to $485.

It was understood by all that Gillis and Cummings were not to travel by train or steamship, and as proof of their progress, the young athletes agreed to obtain a certificate from the mayor or prominent official of each town or city en route, using an agreed-upon list.[3]

On the day before their departure, Gillis and Cumming called on Mr. William Hackett, Mayor of North Sydney, to ask him for a letter of testimonial that they could show to officials of the towns they were to visit. The mayor happily complied, giving a copy to each of the two young adventurers.[4] His words were as follows:

document:

"This is to certify that John H. Gillis and John McDonald are two young men in good standing in athletic circles in the town of North Sydney. They are undertaking to walk across the continent to San Francisco, leaving this town at 7 o'clock a. m. on the 31st day of January, 1906. Their friends bespeak for them the good will of those they may come into contact with en route.

Wm. Hackett,
North Sydney, Jan. 30, '06. Mayor.

Last night a number of friends of the

This is to certify that John H. Gillis and George W. Cumming are two young men in good standing in athletic circles in the town of North Sydney. They are undertaking to walk across the continent to San Francisco, leaving this town at 7 a.m. on the 31st of January 1906. Their friends bespeak for them the good will of those they may come in contact with en route.

Wm. Hackett, Mayor, North Sydney,
Jan. 30, '06

Transcontinental Pedestrians

North Sydney Street, early 1900s

On January 30, merchants of North Sydney joined in a popular public subscription to outfit the two walkers: sweaters, stockings, stout leather leggings, boots, voyageur caps, and military straps for the haversacks. That night friends of the athletes tendered the two young men a farewell banquet at Donald Parker's Queen Hotel, and offered them many wishes of Godspeed for their long journey. In his acknowledgement speech Gillis noted that he and George had made careful plans for the tramp of eight thousand miles. His declaration that they would have to average 22 1/16 miles a day was stated so seriously and mathematically that everyone laughed.

The young men had a map of their route, and planned to follow the Intercolonial Railway to Saint John, the Canadian Pacific to Montreal, the Grand Trunk to Chicago and the Union Pacific to San Francisco. They would use passable highways when such provided a shortcut but many roads were in very bad condition. They intended to travel light, and for pocket money, intended to sell "transcontinental pedestrian" cards for ten cents apiece. Gillis got a chuckle when he reassured his audience, "Don't worry about me, I'll be able to lean on George."

George Cumming made a wry face. "I'll never look up to this guy: he gives me a crick in the neck."

JOHN HUGH GILLIS, born January 2, 1884, was the son of carpenter and cabinetmaker, Angus Hugh Gillis, and his wife, Margaret Ann MacFarlane.[5] John's mother died in 1904; his father had married again and moved to Glace Bay. John Hugh towered at six feet four and a half inches. All the Gillis men were very tall – John Hugh and his father, "Big" Angus, and his brothers, Peter Dan and young Malcolm.

John Hugh loved to run. As a six-year-old, in the Margaree Valley, he chased an errant young sheep, caught it, after some distance, and returned back home carrying the animal. John Hugh was prominent in athletic circles, known as one of the best distance runners in the country. He held the championship of Cape Breton for all distances above five miles. In 1905 he set the Cape Breton record for five miles with a time of 28 minutes, 27 3/5 seconds. Both he and brother Peter Dan used to run to a meet ten miles away and, at the end of the games, run home again.

Margaret Ann Gillis

Angus H. Gillis

John Hugh Gillis (right) in an early family photo

After a year or two at Saint Francis Xavier College, John Hugh dropped out to work as a carpenter. By 1903 he was employed at Revelstoke, British Columbia. The front page of the *Sydney Daily Post* of January 29, 1906, noted,[6] "If there is anybody around this end of the country who can be depended on to finish this long jaunt inside the required time J.H. is the man." Gillis had just turned twenty-two.

So why did John Hugh Gillis, the challenged athlete in this

test of endurance and enterprise, agree to George Cumming as his walking mate? Probably because John Hugh did not want to walk eight thousand or so miles by himself. Perhaps he was taken with George's charm and wit, thinking the man might be an amusing companion in the long months ahead. Furthermore, Cumming was unmarried, and willing to go. John Hugh's other athletic friends were tied to family and jobs.

GEORGE WALKER CUMMING's family had lived in Nova Scotia for three generations. George was born July 2, 1874, at New Glasgow in Pictou County, to John M. Cumming and his wife Annie M. Cameron. John M.'s father, William, immigrated as an infant from Inverness Shire, Scotland, with his parents, who settled at Sunny Brae. William and his wife, Christena Fraser, moved to Piedmont. Four of their sons, including John M., fought for the Union army in the American Civil War. John M. was owner of the Cumming Furniture Factory, maker of and dealer in fine chairs, tables, commodes, bureaus and settees. He served as town councillor for nine years, and as a member of the All-Canada Curling Champions from 1881–1884.[7]

George played hockey and figure-skated. His mother Annie died shortly after his fifteenth birthday. The 1891 census of New Glasgow listed him as sixteen years of age. He is found again in the 1903–1904 Street Directory of Sydney, as a desk clerk at the Minto Hotel (which was electric lit, had livery stables, and located on a busy commercial street with an electric tramway line). George figured prominently in the Steel Works Minstrels and other musical organizations. He was of sturdy build, and chronically overstated his height as five feet and five and a half inches.[8] Unlike his Catholic friends, George belonged to the Methodist Church. Known to his friends as "Punk," he was thirty-one years old when he volunteered to set out on the long walk.[9]

— • —

The two men had no experience of long-distance walking and accepted the draconian terms of the wager naïvely. They not only had to endure winter's cold and storms, and summer's heat and pests, to earn their travelling expenses. Worse still, each man was to come back with the equivalent of a white-collar worker's five month's wages. To be fair, Don Parker, the twenty-six-year-old chief promoter of this scheme, was proud of his athletic young brother-in-law, and was just as naïve in coming up with conditions of the bet. And, to make matters worse, Gillis, intelligent but inexperienced, may have had his own hand in working out the agreement.

On that first frosty morning at the Sydney railway station, George Cumming did not show up, although one local paper, the *Record* asserted that he arrived early but was called away on an emergency.[10] John Hugh Gillis was left alone to embark on the daunting journey, until John "Jack" McDonald, the young physical director of St. Joseph's Amateur Athletic Association, stepped forward after a snap decision and offered to accompany him.

JACK was born at Pictou town October 15, 1885,[11] the son of Donald McDonald, Roman Catholic ship captain and carpenter,[12] and his Baptist wife, Mary Mitchell of Jeddore, Halifax County. The 1891 census lists Donald, age 77 (and the son of parents born in Scotland), as the father of eight children. The 1901 Pictou census showed Mary a widow and young John, 15, a plumber.[13] Mary and her children moved first to Halifax and later to the Sydney area. On September 27, 1904, at Glace Bay, John, nearly nineteen and a boilermaker, married Rosey Beyers, seventeen,[14] who had been born at Lennox, Massachusetts, to carpenter Joseph Beyers and his wife Mary. John, five feet four and three quarter inches in height,[15] was one brother of the well-known McDonald Brothers Acrobatic Trio.[16] One of his acrobatic brothers was Ranald, arrived in Sydney in 1900, to gain fame as a boxer, skater, acrobat, runner and tightrope artist.[17]

McDONALD TAKES CUMMING'S PLACE.

Jack McDonald, who replaced Cummings this morning, starting with Gillis in the ocean-to-ocean tramp, has for the past couple of months been physical director of St. Joseph's A. A. A. in North Sydney. The little fellow is a crack

The *Sydney Daily Post* used the adjective "plucky" as it described the athletes beginning a trek of eight thousand miles under the most restrictive conditions in the dead of winter. A long-distance runner who had never done any long-distance walking! A former hockey player and figure skater who must have gone fairly soft clerking in a hotel and singing in choral groups! A third who knew more about a gymnasium floor than a windswept continent! Not a cent in their pockets. Where would they eat and sleep? Where would they stay when snow storms blocked the path? They were not well clothed for the temperatures of central Maine, and in the spring they would walk quagmire roads and coarse-cindered railway tracks, to be stung by mosquitoes and black flies. And in summer, they faced blazing sun and bad drinking water. What would happen should their feet break down from incessant pounding? No doubt someone back home called it a nutty idea and it was.

The Transcontinental Pedestrians
(Note the misspelling of McDonald)

The First Lap

It was still dark at seven a.m. when Gillis and McDonald began walking down the railroad track. They reached the Junction at 8:15. They marched through the villages along St. Andrew's Channel and reached Long Island Main at 11. There they had lunch with a Mrs. McQuarrie at George's River. She was the first of many generous, and intrigued, citizens who would offer sustenance and/ or lodging to the intrepid travellers.

Having solved the difficulty that delayed his departure, George Cumming telegraphed ahead that he would be leaving Sydney at about 8 a.m. in an effort to overtake the first two walkers.[1] The *Record* reported that Cumming jumped a freight train at Sydney to catch up[2] but this is unlikely because he would have broken the contract by doing so. The *Daily Post* stated that

Cumming walked to the station before Boisdale, and that Gillis walked back four miles to pick him up.[3] The three men then had dinner at a friend's house in Boisdale, and retired to bed after a wearying day.

So now, three men were walking, and they had to get used to walking together on the railroad track. The two shorter travellers could take one cross tie at a time without losing stride, but Gillis as tall as he was, could easily step two ties at a time without stretching or over striding. He was forced to pace himself with his two companions, although, when snow covered the ties, that adjustment was much easier.

As the men travelled along, they chatted about friends, and sports, and about family. John Hugh talked about the beautiful Margaree country where he was born, and where he attended school until he was seven, when his father and mother moved to North Sydney. His great grandfather had immigrated from Morar, on the coast opposite the Isle of Skye, when the managers of the young laird were "reforming" the estate.[4] Anyway, there wasn't enough room on that scratchy Highland ground for big families. John Hugh's father's brother, Malcolm the Bard, stayed in the Margaree, had lots of children, mended watches, taught school, wrote Gaelic nature poetry, and was a champion fiddler. George and Jack talked about their Pictou County boyhoods and Jack reminisced about the famous ship *Hector*, the *Mayflower* of the Pictou County Scots.

The first day of February was cold with a biting wind. Gillis was wearing a light overcoat and Cumming sported a loose sack coat. Jack McDonald had started off in ordinary street clothes. As they faced the icy blast, both Gillis and Cumming realized what bone chill they would have felt without the sweaters, stocking caps and leather leggings they'd received from the merchants of North Sydney. Home-knit mittens felt good on their hands. All three men arrived in time for lunch at Beaver Cove (with a Mrs. R. McNeil). At Shunacadie they sold some cards a friendly printer had made up for them in North Sydney:

TRANSCONTINENTAL PEDESTRIANS
FROM NORTH SYDNEY JAN. 31ST 1906 TO
SAN FRANCISCO, CALIFORNIA, AND BACK
HOME BY JAN. 31ST 1907

These they signed with pencil, or nib pen if an inkwell was available. No one could not afford the new-fangled fountain pens.

At Big Beach and Christmas Island, they explained to the locals who they were and where they were going and how they were financing the trip. Many a clannish Scot found the goodly sum of ten cents or even twenty-five cents to help them on their way.

The three men sent a message to Don Parker that they would stay at the Grand Narrows Hotel through the kindness of Mrs. D.A. McNeil the second night, and Cumming assured him that he had not stolen a ride on a freight train.[5] Mr. Parker went by train to "induce Jack McDonald to return [home]" but, when Jack absolutely refused to do so,[6] he gave him donated outdoor clothing and arranged for him to have a share in the prize.

Donald Parker was concerned about the third man in the venture for several reasons. Jack McDonald was only twenty years old. He had recently accepted the job of physical director of St. Joseph's gymnasium, and he was married. What bothered

Don Parker, too, was that a threesome could easily split along the fault line of two on one side and one on the other. Parker hoped that Gillis as leader of the expedition would insist on the original contract between the promoters and the two walkers, John Hugh and George. Gillis, perhaps unwisely, did not intervene and left the decision to Jack McDonald.

When they left the Grand Narrows Hotel (which boasted that Alexander Graham Bell and Helen Keller had been guests twenty years earlier), the three young men passed a restaurant, the Post Office and Customs, a tannery and a boat-building shop, before pushing on to Iona and points southwest. They listened carefully for a train, before crossing the seven-span railway bridge, and subsequently walked about two miles into a gathering snowstorm. Finally, they found a concert and dance at the local hall, complete with step dancers and fiddlers. All three trekkers joined in the square dances, in addition to enjoying the food and a "wee drap or twa." When the dance broke up, all three were invited to a home where Gaelic was spoken. John Hugh chatted with the family but George and John had to wait until the company lapsed into English.

The next morning's departure was late, following a breakfast of porridge and kippers. The men didn't talk much, possibly due to the discomfort between full stomachs and big heads, not to speak of reluctant legs. There was more snow overnight; the walking was slippery and their feet were sore. They were wearing workmen's boots with thick stiff soles which were not pliable, as they should be, at the big-toe joint. The boots did not even have small cleats to prevent slipping.

After lunch at Orangedale, the travellers puffed a lot walking up the steep grade to spend the night at River Denys, where they were the guests of Councillor McLellan. At dinner they met a fellow guest, a geologist who was interested in nearby Marble Mountain, to the east by Bras d'Or Lake. He showed them a marble sample and told them about another geologist, Nicholas Hunter, who had come to Cape Breton forty years ago, looking for oysters. As Hunter traipsed northeast along the lakeshore to Malagawatch with his nose to the ground, he chanced upon bare marble. He had never seen marble of such unique colour or pattern, and figured that, over hundreds of millions of years, the stone must have fractured and reheated several times. Soon the quarrying of that unusual marble created Marble Mountain village with more than a thousand families. The transcontinental pedestrians recalled seeing similar marble in gravestones and monuments, as well as in a marble-top table of the Empire Hall reading room.

The three men had now travelled 140 miles, an average of 28 miles a day, well ahead of Gillis's projected 22 1/16 miles.

On Monday, the fifth of February, the railway track led them to Port Hawkesbury. A clog of ice over the water stilled the bustling town they had known in summer, with its hundred vessels in the harbour, and smelly fish plants and bustling shipyard. The men stopped at the telegraph office to send a message for the bulletin board of Empire Hall: "Hawkesbury stop. Going strong stop. Mainland bound stop. Transcontinental Pedestrians." They bought liniment for their sore feet and went to call on the mayor to seek his "certificate."

Then it was time to board the steam-powered railway ferry, S.S. *Mulgrave*, for the trip across the Strait of Canso. From the chilly rear deck, they could see the barge that the ferry was towing with its load of railway cars and heavy freight. The crossing was rough. Furniture and objects slid across the deck in the salon. The men sold their transcontinental cards, and gossiped with other passengers about the town of Mulgrave, which initially had lost a third of its population to the "Boston States," but now was picking up fast, what with the railway freight sheds and marshalling yards, and the ferry terminal. And the fishing was good when winter was gone.

On Monday evening, February 5, they arrived in Antigonish[7] and made straight for St. Francis Xavier College, where Gillis knew his way around. They found a bite to eat and then bunks for their weary bones. In the morning they met students, a few of whom were freshmen when John Hugh had attended St. F.X. in 1902–1903.[8] Some remembered seeing that very tall fellow at the indoor meet in November way back in 1902. They remembered seeing those legs winning the high jump.[9]

"How did you come in the quarter mile?"

"Just second," replied Gillis.

Father Jimmy Tomkins, who began teaching at St. F.X. in 1902, remembered Gillis as "intelligent, perceptive; would have made a good parish priest with his leadership qualities."

But John Hugh's love of the old Highland Games had taken him in another direction, although after college he had returned regularly by train, when he was not out west, to compete in the Antigonish Highland Games. He enjoyed casting his body and mind into racing short and far, into jumping and pole-vaulting, and into shot putting and throwing the weight over the bar. A piper himself, he pulsed to the sound of the pipe band. He loved to watch the familiar moves of the Highland fling and the reel and sword dances.

At Antigonish, the three travellers called on Mayor Kirk. He was the first mayor to name John McDonald in the certificate. Interested in how they were financing their trip, the mayor suggested they might do well to sell pencils, telling them: "You know, slates and slate pencils are starting to disappear in town schools and they will eventually in the country schools. Lead pencils are taking their place. And even in stores and offices, unless for official documents, pencils are less of a nuisance than pen nibs and the old ink bottle or well. Why don't you invest in a few dozen pencils while you're here?"

They did, and sold quite a few. Knowing that a person could buy a pencil at a shop for a cent or two, the three walkers preferred not to think of that generous gesture as charity but rather as encouragement or investment in their difficult enterprise.

The *Pictou Advocate* carried an account on page one of the undertaking, mentioning only Cumming and Gillis. The *Antigonish Casket* gave no new information except that the three men had been in town on Monday and Tuesday. As usual, both papers added an s to the Cumming surname. The *Sydney Daily Post* also clocked them in Antigonish.[10]

They had trudged through snow all the way to Merigomish when the *Sydney Express* steamed into the station. While it was stopped there a few minutes, a reporter from the *Sydney Record* hopped off and interviewed them.[11] After the men spoke to the reporter, they made their way four miles south of Merigomish Harbour to Piedmont, thirty miles east of New Glasgow. There George found his cousins, Mr. and Mrs. Don Robertson, who made them feel at home in their big farmhouse. The people of this region were mostly farmers, fishermen, and cranberry boggers. This story appeared in the *Sydney Record*, February 9:

PEDESTRIANS NOW AT NEW GLASGOW

North Sydney Walkers interviewed by Record Representative Yesterday

Gillis, Cummings and McDonald, the three young men who left North Sydney on Wednesday week to walk to San Francisco and back, were at Merigomish when the *Sydney Express* passed that point yesterday and expected to reach New Glasgow early today. To a *Record* representative who was on the train the boys stated that their determination to finish their long tramp had not lagged in the least and they were confident of being able to arrive back in North Sydney within the appointed time. The boys also said that they had become very weary on the first few days of the trip, but that they had now become accustomed to walking as much as twenty-five and thirty miles a day without growing tired. The doughty pedestrians are carrying as little clothing as possible and when seen by the *Record* representative yesterday were without overcoats or bundles of any kind. They are still wearing the stocking caps presented to them on their bidding adieu to North Sydney and have learned to very much appreciate the leggings furnished them.

Pictou County

On Thursday evening, February 8, the travellers arrived in New Glasgow, George's hometown, on the East River. They could see by the houses and shops that this area of Pictou County was still enjoying its long boom. At Stellarton, three miles away, and also on the East River, hundreds of miners employed by the Acadia Company were still producing coal to fuel the steel mills of Trenton, two miles away. The three men took time to find Mayor McDougall of New Glasgow. They also went to visit George's father, whom George had not seen for some time. John M. Cumming was now in his early seventies. By 1898, all his children had left home, and he, a lonely widower, married a woman half his age. Now his household consisted of him, his wife, his mother-in-law and lodgers. George had tea and cookies with his father and then went to the Vendome Hotel[12] to meet his companions.

As they went on their way after an early breakfast, George told his companions a little bit about the town. He explained that the population of New Glasgow was five thousand and almost every family had at least one cow and kept hens. All families stocked beef, pork, flour, potatoes, root vegetables and cordwood for the winter, and the fathers repaired the family shoes and cut their children's hair.

A news story in the *Eastern Chronicle* identifies "the original George Cumming, well known here, a son of John Cumming, Esq., West Side. They greatly enjoyed the trip so far and had a good reception along the line. They wished particularly to thank Mr. and Mrs. Don Robertson for kindness."[13]

On Friday, February 9, their visit to Glengarry Station caused something of a brouhaha when George Cumming wrote to the *Sydney Daily Post* that at Glengarry the boys "had received pretty scurvy treatment from the residents, none of whom would give them a night's lodging or anything to eat, the travellers being compelled to sleep in the railway station without food or covering. Neither would the people sell them anything to eat in the morning and they had to travel to Truro [about two dozen miles] before getting breakfast. This is the only place along the line up to date where the boys were not well received."[14]

The *Truro Daily News*[15] quoted this strong reaction in the *Pictou Advocate*:

Many persons will take the ground that the thrifty, hard working people of Glengarry did a mite right in not encouraging these bum pedestrians. If all people in their line of march would treat them in the same way these young fellows would be compelled to return home and engage in some decent and honest employment.

What an insult it was to Pictonians, who prided themselves on their hospitality! The weekly *Pictou Advocate* printed a strong rebuttal from a resident of Glengarry on the front page:[16]

Although the boys arrived after the supper hour, Mr. Graham provided for them a good meal and gave them a hearty welcome – just what worthy strangers might expect in this settlement. Mr. Graham could not provide sleeping accommodation but the visitors never tried another door. They returned to the railway station where the Agent made them as comfortable as he possibly could, on a lounge and a well-padded table ... If the boys experience no greater discomforts before reaching their destination they will have a pleasant trip.

A report in the *Amherst News*[17] of February 26th on "That Glengarry Affair" was copied in the *Sydney Daily Post* on page two, three days later.[18] The reporter stated "the boys" got up at 6:45 the next morning, had a good wash and walked seven miles to West River for breakfast, evidently not getting along together and "inviting each other to use the road if he did not want to travel in the others' company."

When John Hugh read those newspaper comments, he angrily told George Cumming he was not happy with the ill feeling Cumming had stirred up. No one owed them a meal or a night's lodging. If the men were to be greeted kindly on the way, there must be no more of this. The Glengarry Affair was the beginning of hard feelings between John Hugh and George. John Hugh considered himself the leader of the expedition whereas George, nine years older, thought he had the experience and wisdom to speak his piece. Usually charming and witty, he could be abrasive when crossed.

To offset the unpleasantness, Gillis had a telegram sent from the three of them at Londonderry to Don Parker in North Sydney. They asked him through the *Daily Post* to express their thanks to the many people who had shown kindness to them by putting them up along the route.[19] They should have placated the *Pictou Advocate* as well, but did not because it might show a rift in their ranks.

Before Londonderry, the travellers stayed at the American House in Truro, attended St. John's Church (clad in jerseys and sweaters) and received the required document from Mayor Murray.[20] They had chosen to walk the route around by Truro instead of the briefer distance of the Short Line along the Northumberland Coast – a result of their ignorance of geography. The men later admitted they would "have to learn the short cuts in order to win the wager."[21]

44

Lost in a Blizzard

Snow began to fall, at first gently then in dense curtains. The northwest wind picked up, moving rapidly into gale ferocity. Drifting snow covered the ties and rails, and formed deep banks. All three men found the going hard. The snow was knee-deep. They talked about turning back, but figured they might he about halfway to Wentworth Station. Pulling their caps down to their eyebrows, they turned their collars up. Soon they could not even see where they were going. All was white and windy, and the day was darkening. They held hands so as not to be separated. When one stumbled, the others righted him. If one tired for a time, the others lent him strength. But soon all three became confused by the barrage of snow in their eyes, in a night with no horizon.

They wandered off the track and were walking between pole fences, the tops of which they could barely see. Finally they arrived at what seemed a T-crossroad. Should they go right or straight ahead? Forward, they decided. The snow was now up to their thighs, but they ploughed slowly on. Finally there was a brief lull in the storm. John Hugh turned and saw a light some distance away. The men changed direction, making for possible shelter, waiting, again and again, for a lull to reveal the light again. A farmhouse, God be praised! They knocked. A burly man came to the door. George flashed a snowy grin, "We're the winter scarecrows."

Glancing at those rough-looking, hoary strangers, the man thought briefly, then announced "I don't know."

A little old woman peered around him and said, "Come in, come in, you poor souls! Eddie, get them a broom so they can brush off and take them upstairs to find a change of clothes." She bustled off into the kitchen.

"You're a sight," she smiled when the three came down. John Hugh had on a sweater with sleeves halfway to his elbows and overalls halfway to his knees. George and John seemed to have lost their hands and feet. George, ever the clown, pranced over to the mirror, flapped his sleeves, and said, "Aren't you scared out of your wits?"

"Now," she said, "don't talk till you've had some hot tea. I've opened a big bottle of my chicken and cut thick slices of bread." The tea and jellied chicken, the new bread, and the chocolate cake revived them.

"I'm Mrs. Langille" she said, "and Eddie is my youngest son. And what might your names be?" They introduced themselves and told her how they were walking to San Francisco and back.

"You're codding," Eddie guffawed.

They produced their card. "Well, I never!" she exclaimed. So they told their story.

"You're lucky," Eddie said, "that you saw the lamp we always put in our front window. It's dangerous to be lost in a snowstorm. Some men have died between their house and the barn."

Mrs. Langille told them how her husband's family were Protestants from France away back and he was dead now. Her children, all boys, had moved away, out west or to the States; except Eddie, who didn't care much for school. He stayed with her to run the big farm. Seeing that their eyes were drooping as she talked, she asked her son to show them beds. "You'll find a chamber pot under each bed and it'll be your job to empty them in the outhouse. Good night."

The base burner in the hall had mica windows in the door, through which they could see the white flames of the burning anthracite coal. A long black stovepipe wound its way to the chimney hole upstairs, giving some heat to the halls during the night. Each of the three exhausted walkers sunk into a feather bed, drew up his sheet, blankets and quilt, and fell asleep. When they woke in the morning, they rushed into their clothes. A skim of ice covered the chamber pots. Eddie had a wood fire going in the kitchen stove, and Mrs. Langille served all with smooth porridge that had cooked overnight in the double boiler.

The snow drifted all day. The lane and the road were blocked. The men helped Eddie dig a path to the barn and feed the animals, but, being town boys, they had to let him do the milking. They dug a path to the outhouse. There was nothing else to do but play checkers and read and talk with the Langilles, and give the collie an occasional pat. There were lots of books. John Hugh enjoyed the World Literature set, beginning with myths of Babylon and the Egyptian hymn to Aten.

Mrs. Langille, a good cook, gave them farm-sized servings. The wind died during the day so John Hugh and George and Jack turned out with Eddie and his farm neighbours to shovel and plough the road to Folly Lake. Then it was time for a good supper and early bed.

Wednesday morning, February 14, the Langilles and their visitors were up early for breakfast and a strenuous day ahead. The trio thanked their hosts and offered to pay but Mrs. Langille would not hear of it. They gave her their card as a keepsake and she gave them a noonday lunch to carry away. Down the open road they went to Folly Lake and were happy to see that the railway track had been ploughed.

The sun and warmer weather made the snow heavy to walk through. When they puffed into Oxford Junction, the men decided to continue walking the short distance to Oxford itself. Then they found their way to a boarding house. At dinner they told about their trek and showed their card. After the exclamations died down, their hosts provided some more information about Oxford. It had not been named for Oxford, England, but came about because the river was shallow enough there for ox carts to cross. The Black and Little Rivers provided power for saw and gristmills, and the Philip did so for a woollen mill, owned by the Hickman family, which made wonderful blankets and heavy blanket coats. Great country for farms and wild blueberries and maple syrup!

The next morning was bitterly cold. When a boarder asked them, "Do you know how cold it is?" they shook their heads. "Forty below," he said. "That's unusual but it happens. Oxford is in a bowl with hills around and the cold keeps falling to the bottom. Keep your ears covered and rub your nose and cheeks often." Without such care, the moist cold at that temperature soon froze the ears and the tip of the nose without anyone being aware. One walker would notice and say to the other, "Your nose and ears are white." All three men had to keep their hands moving inside their mittens and stamp their feet to keep them from turning numb. Even the insides of their mouths felt cold. They knew from experience the agony that followed when once inside in a heated building the nose or ears or extremities began to thaw out.

Instead of taking the railroad track, which traced an arc with curlicues, the men followed the straight highway to Amherst. The proprietor of the Amherst Hotel, on well-treed Victoria Street, treated them to a late dinner. The next day citizens cheered them and bought their pencils and souvenir cards as they left for Sackville, ten miles across the windy Tantramar Marshes. On the lovely site of Mount Allison University, the three talked to students and professors, and stirred up enough interest to be invited to the dining hall and to find a place to sleep. They left the next morning at ten o'clock and walked the twelve miles in about three hours to Dorchester, where Mr. Tait, the owner of the Windsor Hotel, treated them to a fine dinner

Moncton Sojourn

A curious crowd welcomed the three when they arrived at the Intercolonial station in Moncton at 8:30 p.m. on Saturday, February 17, after a trek from Sackville of almost forty miles. Telegraphers at the Sackville and Dorchester stations had wired ahead. Mayor Steeves signed a paper certifying their arrival on foot in the city. Patrick Gallagher invited them to stay as guests in his hotel, the Minto. At their request, Mr. Gallagher arranged with Mr. Percy N. Crandall to have pictures taken that night. Mr. Crandall promised to forward the photographs to the Grand Union Hotel in Saint John so that they could have new souvenir cards printed. The men enjoyed a late dinner and were interviewed by a reporter of *The Daily Times.*

Gillis and McDonald went to Mass at St. Bernard's Church on Sunday. Cumming attended service at the Wesley Memorial Church. The Minto Hotel had a livery stable business and Mr. Gallagher got his stableman to drive them around in a horse and sleigh, wherein a buffalo robe covered their legs and laps. They saw the great railway shops of this headquarter town for the Intercolonial Railway which employed several thousand workers. After lunch with Patrick Gallagher, a reporter from *The Moncton Transcript* interviewed them. What follows is part of the long news item in both *The Daily Times*[1] and *The Moncton Transcript*[2] of February 19, 1906:

TRANSCONTINENTAL TRAVELLERS IN MONCTON

John H. Gillis, G.W. Cummings [sic] and John McDonald, the trans-continental travellers, who have undertaken to walk to San Francisco and back inside of a year, for a wager, were registered at the Minto yesterday. The travellers arrived in Moncton at 8.30 Saturday night, having walked from Sackville, a distance of 39 miles, during the day. While in Moncton the travellers were the guests of Mr. P. Gallagher at the Minto by whom they were well looked after.

The travellers left here about 2.30 yesterday afternoon and expected to reach Petitcodiac last night. They expect to reach St. John on Wednesday. While here they were photographed by Mr. P.N. Crandall and they intend acting on a suggestion given them here to have souvenir cards bearing their photographs which they will offer for sale as they journey.

The travellers follow the railroad principally but go by the highway when possible. Before leaving the Minto they returned very hearty thanks to Mr. P. Gallagher for his hospitality during their stay in the city. They expect to return by the same route and stop at the same hotel. The men received their passports from Mayor Steeves Saturday night.

TRANSCONTINENTAL TROTTERS PASS THROUGH MONCTON

George W. Cummings, John McDonald and J.H. Gillis . . . have walked by the I.C. Railway from Sydney to this place, a distance of 338 miles . . . While in the city they attended divine service, Cumming going to the Methodist church and Gillis and McDonald attending services at St. Bernard's Church.

J.H. Gillis is a native of Cape Breton, a fine looking specimen of manhood slightly over six feet in height and is a widely known athlete and long distance runner. McDonald is a native of Pictou, N.S., sturdy but smaller in stature than Gillis, and has been living in Sydney for some years. He is one of the brothers in the well-known McDonald Brothers Acrobatic Trio. George Cummings is a native of New Glasgow but has lived in Sydney since the boom. He is a robust, well-set young man and is talented musically, having figured prominently in the Steel Works Minstrels and other musical institutions in Sydney and neighbouring places. On leaving the *Transcript* man, who wished them bon voyage, Cumming's talent presented itself in the following verses:

Cold winter winds are sweeping
The hillsides white with snow,
And the sad grey skies are weeping
As on and on we go.
Cease, poor skies, your sorrow,
For out of the chill and gloom,
In the smile of another morning,
We'll be back to see you soon.

Here we see a sensitive and touching side to George Cumming.

In a time of strict religious observance when, on Sunday, some conscientious Christians would read only the Bible and certainly not the newspaper, the *Moncton Times* of February 23, 1906, and *The Sydney Record* the next day, carried this fascinating news item:[3]

Made Fuss Over Pedestrians

Considerable fuss was made by a number of church going people of Moncton because of their belief that Gillis, Cummings and McDonald, the North Sydney transcontinental pedestrians, were photographed in a Moncton studio on Sunday. The *Moncton Times*[4] denies that such was the case, however, stating that the boys were photographed by electric light after their arrival on Saturday night. The pedestrians have had their photos put on buttons [sic], which they will sell along their route.

Saint John and Controversy

The men pressed to Saint John, which they reached in two and a half days, a distance of ninety-four miles. They stayed overnight in Petitcodiac. Early Tuesday morning, they stretched out for Sussex, where they stopped at a small hotel. The following day they sold their cards and pencils, and loaded up with sandwiches. They seem to have walked all night and arrived in Saint John in the morning after a tramp of 47 miles. They had made up some lost time in this burst of energy.

Queen's Square, Saint John, ca. 1906

How carefully they were watched and challenged becomes obvious in the next item, carried in three newspapers, the *Saint John Globe* February 22, 1906, *The Moncton Transcript* the next day and *The Sydney Record* on March 1, 1906:[4]

ARE THEY WALKING?

Under the above heading *The Moncton Transcript* of Friday last says:

The three young men, G.W. Cummings, John H. Gillis and John McDonald, of North Sydney, who claim they are walking from St. John to San Francisco and back on a wager, expected to leave St. John yesterday afternoon. They say their route will be from St. John by Montreal and Toronto to Windsor, thence over to Detroit and on to San Francisco. The men say they have walked all the way to St. John. A correspondent of the *St. John Globe* disputes this and declares they bought second-class tickets at Apohaqui and started for St. John on Wednesday morning on the Sussex train. How far they travelled by her he did not know. They put up at the Grand Union about an hour after the arrival of the Sussex train.

Transcontinental Pedestrians

They did indeed register at the Grand Union Hotel. A hundred years later we cannot gather and test the evidence concerning the alleged ride on the railway. If the *Globe* correspondent had named such witnesses as the ticket seller and a passenger or two, we would be sure and sorry. The case lacks a reasonable burden of proof. Would intelligent men take such a chance on the very doorstep of the promoters of the transcontinental walk? Would they not know that a train ride would cause the contract to become null and void? Would they not foresee an inevitable return to their homes, hanging their heads in shame?

After cleaning up and having lunch, they explored the port city, and the North Market wharf where sailing ships were laid up for the winter. They saw in the distance the high, rocky cliffs and lighthouse of Partridge Island, where many quarantined Irish immigrants had died. They visited the old city market on Charlotte Street and the old courthouse with its amazing spiral staircase. As soon as their photographs arrived from the Crandall Studio in Moncton, the men visited a local printer and had a quick job done on their new souvenir cards. They seem to have had some trouble getting a certificate from the mayor of Saint John, who was either out of town or tied up with business or family matters.

Nevertheless, the trio did attract considerable attention in the port town. Here is part of the long news story about the three on the front page of the *Evening Times*, Saint John, February 21, 1906.[5]

WILL GO TO 'FRISCO IF ROADS ARE GOOD

Three Transcontinental Pedestrians in Town

STARTED FROM SYDNEY

And Must Make Trip in a Year and a Day?

Trip Made on Wager?

Must Earn Two Hundred Each

Three burly looking individuals, wearing broad blue tams, brown leather gaiters and dark suits, strolled into the Grand Union Hotel this morning and registered as G.W. Cummings, John H. Gillis and John McDonald, North Sydney, "Intercontinental Pedestrians." The three young men are on a tour from Sydney to 'Frisco and back, having pledged themselves under a wager to cover the entire distance on foot, and land in North Sydney in 366 days with two hundred dollars each. The wager is put up by six well-known sporting men of North Sydney.

The trio started out from North Sydney, penniless, on January 30 and showed a *Times* man a certificate from the Mayor of the town. They carry little or no luggage and sell lead pencils and souvenir cards. They left Sussex yesterday noon at four o'clock arriving here about ten this morning and they will start out again tomorrow.

The Saint John *Globe* of Saturday February 24 reported their departure from the city:[6]

STARTED AGAIN

After a two days' stay in the city, the three "transcontinental travellers" from North Sydney, C.B., who are to walk from their home to California and back on a wager of $1,200, left for more westerly fields on Friday morning. From the city to Fairville they took the King's highway, but on reaching the latter point got beyond the trespass signs and took to the C.P.R. track, which they will follow to Montreal, there taking the Grand Trunk for Chicago. Speaking with manager Robertson of the Fairville Bank of New Brunswick branch, who hails from their home town, the travellers said their greatest delay so far had been caused by the time consumed in obtaining the signatures of the mayors of incorporated towns. This was a difficulty here.

North to McAdam

They were up with the crows on that Friday morning, February 23, 1906. After a quick breakfast, the walkers headed north. Finding it hard going in the snow, they slept at Welsford, by the Nerepsis River, on a flat plain surrounded by snowy hills. As they left, they saw an old covered bridge on the road over the river. By the time they reached Blissville they were so hard put that they laughed when George quipped, "I'd be glad to exchange the bliss of Blissville for the bliss of Fredericton Junction." They found something to eat at the Junction but had to spend the night in the station house.

Stiff and sore after a poor sleep, they started west again. When they strode into McAdam, the men were amazed by the huge three-storey station house-hotel owned by the Canadian Pacific Railway. They gulped and looked around, but saw no alternative even if the chateau was too expensive for them. They explained their mission to the hotel manager and told him about the wager, and about how they were financing their long walk. They asked in the circumstances whether he might give them a special deal on sleeping arrangements for all three men in one room.

Intrigued by the adventure of these intrepid young men, the manager asked, "Would you mind sleeping and eating in the staff quarters?"

"Thank you," they said, relieved. "You're very kind." They had a late dinner, at which the hotel employees could not hear enough of the long tramp of these men, one so tall compared with his chums, indeed, compared with anyone else in the room. The staff were proud of their hotel, which they said had been built five years earlier of local granite.

CPR Station Hotel, McAdam

Sunday morning, the travellers learned sadly that the previous day, Moncton's huge railway shops, the town's mainstay, had been destroyed by fire in two and a half hours. Five acres of buildings burned, car shops, brass foundry, boiler-making shops, electric light plant. Half a mile of blazing cars scattered over the great railway yard. Worst of all, one man had died and still others were unaccounted for. Cumming, McDonald and Gillis remembered well the railway men they had talked with in Moncton.

Fire at Intercolonial Railway shops, Moncton, N.B.,
February 24, 1906

An assistant cook prepared sandwiches for them Tuesday, and the hotel manager bid them Godspeed. They went into the station to procure a timetable, so at least they would know when passenger trains were coming – they would have to look and listen carefully for the freight trains.

At one o'clock Tuesday, February 27, the men spotted a flag with 13 stripes and 46 stars, which they counted as an idle exercise. At Vanceboro, the customs port of entry, they showed the officer their credentials and the certificate from the mayor of North Sydney. They certainly had nothing to declare. They strolled briefly around that booming railway town on the St. Croix River and talked with people in the shops and the station, letting George, with his charm and verbal skills, manage the sale of souvenirs. It was twenty below zero (–29°C), although from the snow depth, they judged this was good snowshoeing country. Collectively they agreed it would be great to have snowshoes, which, however, along with moccasins and very heavy socks would require money they did not have. The men were so tired that night they were glad to find bunks in a nearby lumber camp.

At Forest City they saw men ice fishing on Grand Lake. High up an eagle wheeled and then shot down like an arrow to be lost from sight. At one point, a huge moose crashed through the brush, scowled at the men and turned away.

The March 3, 1906 issue of the *Sydney Daily Post* headlined:[7]

TRANSCONTINENTAL PEDESTRIANS

Expect to be in Montreal in Two weeks

Heard from in Forrest, Maine

Don Parker, of North Sydney, received a letter last night from J.H. Gillis, one of the three men on the ocean to ocean tramp, dated February 27th, Forrest, Maine. The boys are in good health and still plodding along on their journey. They expect to be in Montreal in about two weeks from the date of writing. The pedestrians feel pretty sore over the reports in the New Brunswick papers to the effect that they rode part of the distance between Moncton and St. John on a train. This statement is a canard pure and simple, an old dodge (as Gillis puts it) of the newspapermen to get copy.

If they had intended to cover any part of the distance by rail, it is certain that the trick would not be tried so near home. They would have waited until they got farther along in the States, as such a breach, if committed near the border as stated, would be sure to reach the promoters of the tramp, the men who put up the money, and the affair would be called off.

In conclusion, they wished, through the columns of *The Post*, to thank all those people who have so kindly given them assistance along the route, and hope that the next message they send will be from Montreal.

George Cumming wrote[8] to the sporting editor of the *Post* that when the sale of pencils did not bring in enough cash, the irrepressible "Punk" impersonated the voice and gesture of William Ewart Gladstone, Prime Minister of Great Britain, and so tickled the fancy of the crowd that they passed over the shekels. George wished to be remembered to his Sydney friends, especially Nelson Kennedy, Harry Mersereau and Pius McMullin.

Danforth, farther on and a little bigger, also enjoyed being located on one of Maine's multitude of lakes, East Grand Lake. Lying in their bunks, the men could hear night noises: the ice on the lake cracked and rumbled as it buckled in the dropping temperature, trees groaned and creaked, a lone fox barked in the distance and coyotes howled eerily. Lulling sounds for a deep sleep!

Maine Snow Storms

On Wednesday the 28th of February they found shelter from a violent snowstorm in the station house at Kingman, and went cold and hungry for twenty-four hours. They paced up and down, swinging their arms and stamping their feet. They felt the pains of empty stomachs. All three tried sleep at times, but were too cold and miserable. To pass the time, they reminisced about family, sports, books and everything that came into their heads. George got on John Hugh's nerves; he hogged the conversation and told blatant whoppers, describing at length talking to Wilfrid Laurier, the prime minister. Finally after many hours, the men began to sing at the top of their voices. At last some residents noticed their plight and brought them meat and biscuits, plus a can of salmon, which they saved all the way to Montreal against future famine.[9]

Next they travelled to Mattawamkeag, situated on the river of the same name, in what looked like a frozen marsh with lowland evergreens and shrubs in white coats. They sold cards and pencils for enough money to enable them to settle in at a small hotel for a square meal and warm beds.

The cold wind howled from the northwest and hard snowflakes swirled through the trees. The three men thought a storm might be coming but they could not be sure. They felt they had to press on or they would fall farther behind in their schedule. Ravens rode the air currents and red squirrels seemed to be unperturbed. After about an hour's tramping, they noticed trees swaying and making shot-like sounds. Snow fell from a grey sky, piled up and swirled into deep drifts. The fine granular crystals stung their faces like nettles. The roar of the wind through the trees sounded like a coming train, so they stopped and listened, then plunged on. Travelling down the tunnel of the track, they were forced to lift their feet high and set them down firmly in the thick snow. Silently they willed themselves forward, groping fearfully across the railway bridge over the river far below. Then they saw lights ahead and found new strength. A station house, but the sign was covered with snow. The stationmaster told them they were in "Brownville Junction. You'd better brush off the snow and rest a while. When you catch your breath, the hotel is across the street."

The storm raged on. Brownville was snowbound. The hotel and the town were full of men: railway men, quarry men, miners, foundry men, lumbermen. George, Jack and John Hugh spoke with all of them at length in the dining room and the lounge. They told of their long walk so far through all the rigours of winter and of their plans to walk to San Francisco and back. They sold many pencils and souvenir cards to sympathetic workmen who had money in their pockets. For a pencil they got nothing less than twenty-five cents, and in one case five dollars.

The travellers heard much about the area and the work the men did. Some quarried slate. Others worked for the Katahdin Iron Works. Most of them did hot labour at the stone blast furnace. The lumbermen stripped the wood off the mountains to make charcoal in the kilns. The cast iron went elsewhere to make rails.

A Bridge Too Many

Sunday morning, the 4th of March, the storm had cleared and the temperature had dropped overnight to thirty degrees below zero (-34C). The trekkers covered their ears and rubbed their noses and cheeks to stave off frostbite. As they left, they could see Mount Katahdin, Maine's highest mountain, that large granite mass covered in snow, rising 5,200 feet above sea level. They also saw the tracks of deer, and wondered what chance those gentle creatures would have when ravenous wolves lurked not far off.

With Boarstone Mountain behind them, the men trudged along, passing an octagonal water tower. Pushing around a bend, they came to the spectacular Onawa Trestle. It stretched 1,100 feet long, almost two-thirds of a mile, over the Ship Pond Stream 138 feet below. A CPR sign warned: DANGER! PEDESTRIANS DO NOT CROSS. But what else could they do? Their road was the railway and the only way to the railroad town of Onawa was by those tracks.

Mount Katahdin, Maine

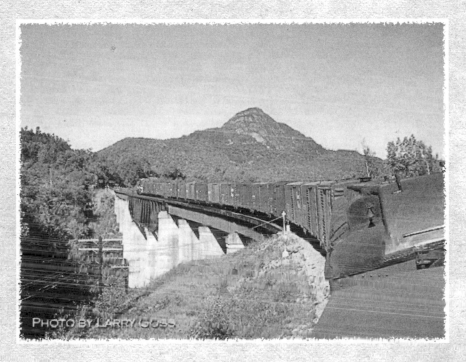

Onawa Trestle, Maine

The men were halfway across the bridge when suddenly they saw a freight train coming around the bend ahead. There was no stand-off, so they were forced to hang on for dear life to the steel apron of the bridge, their legs dangling towards that frozen rocky stream far below.[10] Their taut arms ached as dozens of freight cars clanked and rumbled slowly by. Each minute was torture. At last the three young athletes were able to pull themselves back up onto the bridge, where they collapsed, half-frozen, on the track, shaking and trembling all over. Then they made their way to Onawa Station and found shelter in the small hotel.

Lumber Camp Shelter

On Monday, the fifth day of March, now in the Maine Highlands, the pedestrians came to Greenville at the southern tip of Moosehead Lake, which they were told was the largest lake in Maine. Here was the beauty of Squaw Mountain, Wilson Pond and the nearby isles. To the north were the great woods. Sixty miles to the west was Canada. Snow was falling heavily again and Jackman Station seemed too far away. The men turned north on a tote road in the hope of finding shelter in a lumber camp.

Soon they came to the Kellogg Lumber Company and were welcomed by hearty men at the log-built dining room and kitchen. The big room, heated by a large wood-burning range, was furnished with tables and benches, sideboards and shelves, all of rough lumber. A boarded-off corner with a canvas portiere provided a bunkroom for the cook and cookees. The visitors were so hungry they accepted a second helping of pork and beans on a tin plate with hunks of bread to soak up the gravy. They must have thought they'd died and gone to heaven.

After dinner all headed for the bunkhouse built from unpeeled logs. Rough board bunks filled each wall. Duffel bags and clothes hung on nails at each bunk. Round the stove, with its rack above for drying stockings and mittens, the men gladly gave up their usual pastimes of whittling or poker for an evening with the visitors. As they answered the questions of the curious loggers, the travellers were kidded, "How many times did you hitch a ride on a freight train?"

George, the joker, laughed and shot back, "How many times did you beat your wife? Those freight trains must have been awfully slow because we've been going since the last day of January."

A lumberjack from the Gaspé named Aucoin took out his fiddle and played a reel. He passed it and the bow to John Hugh, who had shown an interest. Gillis played a Gaelic lament he had learned from his uncle Malcolm and a reel he had learned from his father, Big Angus. Then he took out his chanter and gave them a bagpipe air without the pipes. Jack McDonald was prevailed upon to show a little of his acrobatic skill. He did a somersault and a handstand, then walked about on his hands. George Cumming sang the *Skye Boat Song* and led the gang in an all-out rendition of *Clementine* and *I've Been Working on the Railroad*. At last the wayfarers settled into spare bunks on mattresses of ferns and small fir boughs and prayed that the liberally applied talcum powder they smelled would keep the lice away.

They rose early Tuesday after an uncomfortable night and washed and shaved at the sideboard by the back door. What should they do with the water? Toss it out the door, of course, where it froze before it hit the ground. The great, freezing out-of-doors was their toilet. The cook gave them a big helping of fried sausages and potatoes with steaming tea. They thanked the boss and the cook and waved goodbye to the men. Down the tote road to the railway tracks they strode, feeling strong and well nourished.

They passed lakes the Maine people call ponds and stopped at Jackman Station for lunch at a restaurant where they could see the Moose River, too frozen to do its rafting work. A great place to snowshoe and to hunt moose, they agreed. Passing many private logging roads, they reached Holeb, also on the Moose River, with the Attean and Sally Mountains behind it. The Holeb Falls were tamed by the cold.

Eastern Townships

They said farewell to Maine and said hello to the Eastern Townships of Quebec as they stopped at the Canadian border and showed their credentials. They came to Megantic after many hills and curves and a meeting of two trains. They found this to be a lumbering and farming area filled with many Scots, who had settled it twenty years before on the shore of Lake Megantic and in the shadow of Megantic Mountain. They spent the evening writing home. George Cumming sent a letter[11] to the *Post*, saying that they had trudged through two recent snowstorms. "Gillis's feet are beginning to go bad on him and are very sore but he is not holding us back."[12]

Wednesday, they passed through the peaceful little village of Milan, situated on the side of a hill. Gillis had awakened with pains in his heels and a dull ache in the arches of his feet. After walking a short distance, however, his feet felt better. They stopped for lunch at Scotstown. The three hikers talked with people, told their own story, sold their souvenirs and learned about the history and development of this little town. Scots from the Hebrides, actually from the Island of Lewis where there were few trees, had settled here to become lumberjacks, just as the farmers of Hanover, Germany, had become able fishermen and sailors at Lunenburg, Nova Scotia, responding to the power of environment and the need to earn a living. Two things brought this settlement about: the formation of the CPR line through the Townships and Maine to Saint John, and the presence of waterfalls. The Glasgow Canadian Land Trust decided to build a village, and John Scott, the company owner, who gave the settlement its name, built a dam on the Salmon River, a sawmill, an inn for travellers and houses for workers. Gradually they stripped large tracts, the topsoil of which washed away. Already some settlers were turning to dairying.

On Thursday, March 8, the travellers arrived in the lumber town of Bury with its mixture of English, Irish and American residents. The men walked through snow-covered farm and forest and across the Ascot River bridge at Johnville. They learned that Cookshire was a Loyalist town and that Captain John Cook, who received a large grant for farming, had given the town its name. They saw St. Peter's Anglican Church, where John Henry Pope was baptized, married and buried. They also saw his mansion. The people of Cookshire remembered their late, most famous citizen with a plaque; Farmer, banker, exploiter of lumber, copper and gold, militia major, federal minister of agriculture and then of railways and canals.

At last the men came to Bishop's University in Lenoxville,

hoping that the students and professors might be interested in tales of their adventure, in their planned continental trek and in the souvenir cards they were selling to finance it. They found a dining room and makeshift arrangements for their overnight sleep. When John Hugh had a hot shower the next morning, his aching feet felt better. After a breakfast of toast, eggs and bacon, and milk, they walked to nearby Sherbrooke and made the front page of the *Sherbrooke Daily*.[13]

ARE TRAMPING TO SAN FRANCISCO
Three Transcontinental Pedestrians in Town
ON WAGER OF $1200 ARE TO MAKE RETURN TRIP IN YEAR

Three young men from North Sydney, C.B., who term themselves "Transcontinental Pedestrians," are in town today. Their names are G.W. Cumming, J.H. Gillis and John McDonald.

They state that on a wager of $1200 they are walking to San Francisco, Cal., and return, the whole trip to be completed within one year. They state that in order to accomplish this they must average 22 1/16 miles daily. When they arrived at St. Johns, [sic] N.B., their average was less than 18 miles. They have picked up since, and at Sherbrooke their average is 21 miles. The weather has been unfavourable in some respects, and when spring and summer come they expect to be able to step out in a manner to bring the average up and beyond the required figure.

They spent some time finding the home of the mayor in order to get his certificate and strolled around the lovely town, situated at the convergence of two rivers in an area of valleys and hills. The men spoke with people on the street and sold souvenir cards and pencils.

Strathcona Square, Sherbrooke, Quebec

On Saturday, March 10, the trekkers arrived at Magog, located at the northern tip of Lake Memphremagog with a mountain as a backdrop. This was a working people's town: Dominion Textile the major player.

Monday morning, March 12, Gillis rubbed his aching heels and insteps before dressing. Overuse of his feet and his rigid and now worn boots had caused a painful condition (which we know today as plantar fasciitis), an inflammation of the band of thick connective tissue running from heel to the ball of the foot.

The men pressed on and came to Farnham, on the Yamaska River, a major stop on the Canadian Pacific Railway from Montreal through Maine to Saint John. Here the three trekkers stepped into the three-storey station house (with tower) and talked with town residents waiting for the Montreal train. The CPR employed hundreds of men on the trains, in maintenance and repair, and in the manufacture of rolling-stock parts.

Montreal

On Wednesday, March 14, the station agent at Delson advised the three Cape Bretoners not to continue on the CPR track towards Montreal because the long St. Lawrence Bridge from Caughnawaga to La Salle was a busy single-track railway unsafe for pedestrians. If they were not killed on that bridge, they might well be arrested for trespassing. Instead, he suggested, they should walk a dozen or so miles east along the South Shore road to the Victoria Bridge. Accordingly, they tramped through La Prairie de la Magdeleine, admiring views of the St. Lawrence River and the skyline of Canada's then-largest city, Montreal. Gillis tried not to limp as they hiked on the public sidewalk of the two-mile-long Victoria Bridge and then made their way to the Bonaventure Station of the Grand Trunk Railway. The *Sydney Daily Post* reported in its Sporting News:[14]

NO. SYDNEY BOYS
IN MONTREAL

Walking to San Francisco on a Wager

Satisfied with Results

MONTREAL, March 14 – Bronzed by the sun and frosty winds after 31 days actual tramping, three young Nova Scotians, G.W. Cummings, J.H. Gillis and John McDonald, trudged into Montreal today, having walked all the way from North Sydney, a distance of close to a thousand miles. While satisfied with their progress so far, they are determined to press on to San Francisco, and after seeing Mayor Ekers tomorrow, will set out Saturday morning for the west, taking the Grand Trunk route to Chicago, after which they will work further south. These young men hope to get to San Francisco and back in 366 days on a $1,200 wager. They are so far satisfied with results, and show credentials to indicate they have walked the entire distance. They have been actually 43 days on the road, but on account of the storms and bad roads only made progress 31 days.

The three voyagers asked where they might find an inexpensive hotel, as a curious crowd of waiting passengers and others gathered round. The transcontinental pedestrians had to tell something of their story. One man cracked, "Give us the long and the short of it." Some in the crowd laughed, others groaned.

George retorted sharply, "The short of it is we walked all the way from Cape Breton and the long of it is we're walking a longer way still to San Francisco. In short, would you like to come along with the long and the short of us?"

There were no takers. Somewhat mollified, the trio answered questions and seemed to satisfy all, from their weather-beaten and tramp-like appearance, that they had indeed walked so far through the best and the worst of winter weather. They explained that they were paying the expenses of their long walk by selling pencils and souvenir cards, which they passed around. Soon they had made quite a sale. A young Irishman named Liam O'Connor volunteered to show them to a reasonably priced hotel that was "not a far piece."

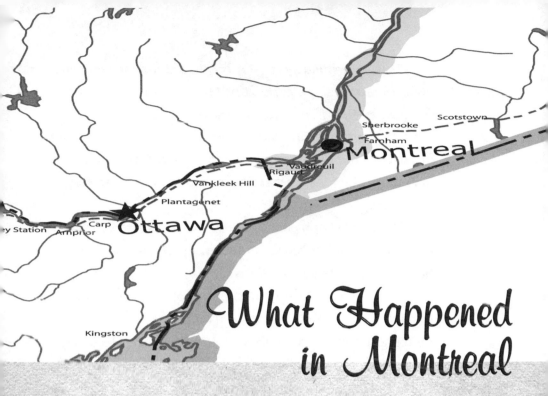

What Happened in Montreal

A Modest Hotel

Liam O'Connor, a black-haired, blue-eyed young man with just a hint of plumpness in face and body, led them along rue Saint-Antoine, all the while full of chat and good humour.

I work on the docks when the port's open but I have a job over the winter in my uncle's hotel in Quebec City. I'm just back here for the long weekend. There's this hotel down by the piers that doesn't cost much and yet it's very decent. It's called "Hotel Cecil" and its owner is Madame Bougeant and as you can guess by the name of the hotel she knows enough English to get along. She caters mostly to sailors and travelling salesmen and bachelor longshoremen like me. Now don't worry, Mrs. Bougeant makes sure her beloved hotel doesn't harbour lice or fleas at all at all. Bad cess to áem!

"This is a busy port," he continued. "Last year over eight hundred ships arrived at Montreal and quite a few brought people from other countries. You'll hear a lot of French and other languages down this way. How's your French, by the way? Just like mine, ha, ha. You'll be looking out on Jacques Cartier Basin and beyond that, the St. Lawrence.

"Mind the slippy snowbank at the crossing! Now we're coming to a famous street, 'the Main,' whose real name is St. Lawrence Boulevard. In a way it's a bit of a dividing line between ordinary French people and ordinary English people. Some say it's a wild place. Now if we turn down here, we go to the foot of the Main. Two blocks east and here we are at Hotel Cecil. Now," he said, taking a breath, "I'll just go in and introduce you."

Liam approached the desk and addressed the dark-haired woman who greeted him with a smile.

"Mrs. Bougeant, these lads are from Nova Scotia and they're walking across North America. Be good to them! Now, fellows, you need some rest. If you like, I'll look in on you the day after tomorrow right after noon dinner. I'm tied up until Saturday. Hey, wait a minute! Would you like to go to the final game of the Stanley Cup on Saturday night?"

They agreed enthusiastically. "All right, I'll get the tickets." And off he went, smiling and nodding at all he passed.

St. Lawrence Boulevard
("the Main") & St. Catherine
Street, Montreal, c.1905

The three Cape Bretoners registered while the owner informed them of the rates: one dollar a day for the room, 15 cents for breakfast, 25 cents for dinner and 20 cents for supper. Cumming and McDonald asked for a room with twin beds and Gillis asked if there was a room with a long bed. Madame Bougeant told John Hugh that one room had a bed for extra tall men like Vikings and she showed the men to rooms on the third floor with a common bathroom down the hall.

Gillis sat down on the long cot, took off his boots and socks and rubbed the swollen, aching soles of his feet as he looked around. Against one wall was an old commode on which sat a large white porcelain basin and ewer. Beside it, a mirror pivoted on a square carved stand, a covered soap dish and a mug. A towel of unbleached linen hung on a side rack. Against another wall stood a tall maple wardrobe, the open door of which revealed wooden hangers on a metal bar. Near the window, with its yellow cotton curtains and interior shutters, were two uncomfortable-looking chairs with horsehair seats. A light bulb hung from the centre of the ceiling. The switch was far from the bed, over by the door.

Six o'clock and time for supper. The three men went down together to the big dining room and, once seated, noticed there were thirteen around the table. Some of the burly men laughed about it but one or two looked a bit anxious. "Somebody's luck will turn bad or there'll be a falling out," one rumbled under his breath.

The aroma of "bubble and squeak" pancakes turned all minds to empty stomachs. An English dish of cooked potatoes, cabbage, onion, eggs and butter beaten together with salt and pepper to form patties, and then fried brown in a skillet, was a favourite with the men. Naturally the diners were curious about the newcomers and were all ears about the big bet. Some thought it was a tough assignment. "The guys who put up the pot have had the best of you."

One noticed that Gillis limped a little when he came in the room. John Hugh told him, "I've had some foot trouble[1] but we'll do it."

And Jack added proudly, "We've come this far since January 31st with only pencils and souvenir cards to pay our expenses."

After the apple pie had raised the comfort level even more, a number of the diners bought the cards and pencils the transcontinental pedestrians just happened to have had in their pockets. A few gathered in the lobby to chat with the "Down Easters." John Hugh went to bed early but his chums decided to explore the lures of the Main, about which they'd heard so much.

Mayor Ekers' Hospitality

Gillis got cleaned up that Thursday morning and had a breakfast of ham and eggs, toast and jam and tea. It felt good. His two companions were still in bed. Gillis used the hotel telephone in the front hall to make an appointment with Mayor Henry Acker Ekers,[2] explaining their mission and their need of the mayor's certificate confirming their arrival in Montreal. Mr. Ekers said he would be at his brewery at 2115 St. Lawrence Boulevard for a short while at one o'clock and could see them there.

The three met the mayor, who had just taken office the first of February.

He would be the last Anglophone mayor of Montreal. Interested in the experience of these young athletes, the mayor gave them more time than they had expected. He also surprised them by introducing a young plainclothes detective, whom he had asked to show them around the city. They went to Vieux Montréal around Notre-Dame and St-Jacques Streets, and absorbed the history and beauty of the Église Notre Dame, the exquisite stained glass windows of its Baptistry and the wood-carving and painting of its chapel of the Sacred Heart. They had a tour of McGill University, the Windsor Hotel and, at cross streets, felt the blast of cold air coming down from Mount Royal. That evening John Hugh rested his feet and wrote letters home while George and Jack went out for the nightly excitement of the Main.

Advice for Sore Feet

The next morning, while his chums were sleeping it off, John Hugh walked over to the clubhouse of the Amateur Athletic Association on Mansfield Street and had a talk with the physical director, a greying man of athletic build. John Hugh told him about the long walk of the transcontinental pedestrians and described his foot trouble after the first month. How was it that he had developed sore, inflamed soles and heels when his companions got off Scot-free?

> *"Are you a runner?"*
>
> *"Yes, I've run the five mile quite often as well as other shorter distances."*
>
> *"That accounts for it. I was a runner and I've had the same trouble. I guess our feet weren't made for such punishment. That thick cushion that runs from the heel to the*

ball of the foot gets inflamed from overuse as it stretches too much. The soreness in the heel and the aching pain in the arch are worse first thing in the morning. Sometimes when I get out of bed, I walk like a duck."

"It can also happen if you wear worn-out boots or ones that are too stiff or don't have room for your toes when they spread as your foot lands. Or if you wear socks that don't take up the sweat, like cotton socks, or get soaked. Or, often, if you have flat feet. But it's mostly the everlasting pounding when you run or, now, when you walk long distances day after day."

"You mean to say," said John Hugh, "that even though you quit running some time ago, you still have this misery?"

"I let it get chronic and now I have to manage it," the physical director replied. "I rub my feet to warm the arch. I roll a ball back and forth under my foot. I sit with my feet elevated. I apply ice or hot compresses. And I put my shoes under the bedclothes at night so they'll be warm in the morning."

John Hugh gave him a worried look. "So what do you advise in my case?"

"Those boots look pretty cracked and stiff. Get a new pair that have enough room for spreading toes and that bend forty-five degrees at the ball. You might ask the shoe clerk about getting arch supports. Wear heavy wool socks that take up the sweat. You're an athlete. You know how important it is to warm up for an event: so walk slowly the first ten minutes. One thing is certain: rest is the most important cure. Get all the rest you can. You should really lay up in Montreal for the next two weeks. Walking across the continent is hardly the prescription *for healing those feet of yours."*

"I guess not," John Hugh agreed, "but there's this wager and I'm committed. It's a test of endurance and determination. I can't quit now."

"Well, slow down a while and make it up when your feet are right. You'll have to manage it. As I do every day," the physical director said ruefully. "If you take it easy and try some of my suggestions, you could see improvement in six weeks or so. Good luck!" he said, shaking John Hugh's hand vigorously.

The Break-up

George and Jack got out of bed in time for noon dinner, feeling the chill of Gillis's disapproval. Finally John Hugh thawed a bit and told them what he had learned about his sore feet. They expressed sympathy and suggested he take it easy in Montreal for a while. "We can't afford the time," John Hugh said, and reminded them they were to go to a printer that afternoon and have more souvenir cards made up.

The other two looked at each other and then Jack blurted out, "We've decided to stay in Montreal for a few days. We're going to chuck this long tramp. It isn't worth the hardship. Why don't you do the same – especially with your sore feet."

John Hugh was shocked, "When did you two decide on this?" Unable to hide his disappointment, he turned to George and said, "When you signed up I was sure you were in it for all the bad weather and the dangers and the satisfaction of doing the nearly impossible."

"It is impossible, John. We were naïve to accept those conditions. Now that we're here, Jack and I are having some fun and we're going to stay a while."

"But we can't give up," said John Hugh, "regardless of the conditions. That would be a lack of sand."

"What do you mean, lack of sand?"

"Grit, determination. We've made a commitment to others and to ourselves. Listen," John Hugh pleaded, hoping against hope they were doing it for the sake of his feet, "you don't need to hold back on my account. You can go on at your own speed and I'll try to catch up to you when my feet are better."

"No, it's not that," said George. "We're tired of the awful grind and just want to have some fun for a change."

John Hugh shook his head. He told them he was concerned about their health, what with all their carousing and womanizing.

Jack exploded, "Why don't you mind your own bloody business? We can look after ourselves."

"Pupa Gillis," said George scornfully, "we hate to disobey your elevated majesty but we're sticking around this den of iniquity."

"In that case," replied John Hugh, unable to control his anger, "our partnership is broken as of now. You can go or stay where you damn well please. I'm heading for Vancouver." He told them he'd notify Don Parker of the change of plans.

George and Jack said they would proceed to Toronto to see Canada's other big city and be back in North Sydney by late May. John Hugh walked away in disgust.

John Hugh was a typical young man of his time, brought up in a closely-knit family with strong religious ties. Athletic performance depended on a healthy body and a focused mind. He was disgusted that his companions sapped their strength and damaged their health by indulging in the Montreal nightlife. John Hugh was fond of women but his late mother had raised him to respect them.

That afternoon Gillis sent a telegram to Don Parker, informing him that he had broken with his two companions, who had decided to stay a while in Montreal. He asked Parker and the other promoters to agree to his going solo to Vancouver instead of to San Francisco. John Hugh then went to a photographer and had his picture taken for a rush order of souvenir cards with only his photograph on them. At the Henry Morgan store on Phillips Square he bought flexible boots with good toe room for five dollars, and some arch supports and woollen socks.

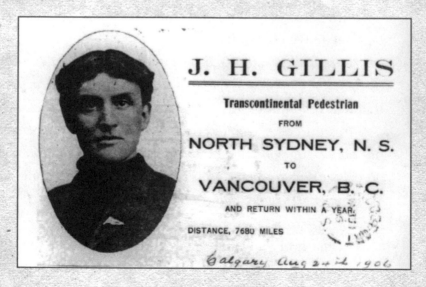

One of Gillis's souvenir cards

Saturday Afternoon Outing

On Saturday, Liam arrived at the hotel wearing a green cap, a loud green scarf and a shamrock pinned to his coat. He noticed that the three travelling companions were looking a bit glum. George drew a long face. "What's with the green, Liam? Is it St. Patrick's Day?"

"Faith, how did you guess?" replied Liam. He offered to show them some of the town and to help them shop for a few essentials.

W.H. Scroggie department store, Montreal

The three decided to set aside their differences for the day and take advantage of Liam's offer. They rode in an electric streetcar and went west on St. Catherine Street until, at the corner of University, they came to the department store of W.H. Scroggie,[3] where they bought woollen socks, shirts and underwear. They also purchased apples at Scroggie's grocery department. They wandered around the great store of Henry Morgan and Company at 2185 St. Catherine and bought green scarves. As they strolled through the shops, and along the snow-banked sidewalks, they heard both French and English, saw buildings of eight storeys and more and felt the excitement of a great city of three hundred thousand people.

Snow banks on Sherbrooke Street, Montreal

Passing the Ouimet Theatre they saw a poster advertising a "photographic play: *The Great Train Robbery*" – five cents for an afternoon showing. Keenly interested, they trooped in. Soon the broad beam of light hit the white screen and flickering images appeared.

The audience was spellbound as two masked men entered a railway station and forced the operator to telegraph the engineer to stop the train to take on water. Four bandits boarded the train, shot the mail-car clerk, blew the safe, lined up the passengers along the track and robbed them. They forced the engineer to uncouple the passenger cars, then dropped off the train to their tethered horses. The young daughter of the operator found her father, and untied him. He ran to a square dance and organized an immediate posse. The pursuit was relentless, and all of the bandits were killed.

Liam and his three friends came out of the theatre blinking after watching the jerky black and white images. They agreed that this wonderful invention had made a lot happen in ten minutes.

Stanley Cup Final

That night they went to see the second game of the two-game finals for the Stanley Cup in the eight-year-old Arena at the corner of St. Catherine West and Wood Avenue.[4] Liam soon informed them that the Montreal Wanderers were not playing up to their usual form. In the first half the Ottawa team skated like rough demons around the Wanderers' net. The goalie Ménard made great saves. The paralysed defence began to lift the puck into the benches in order to get breathing space. Bob

Meldrum, the referee, warned them and finally sent Strachan to the penalty box. The first half ended 3 to 1 for the visiting team. During the intermission Liam regaled his friends with local hockey history.

The Montreal Wanderers, 1905

"The Irish Canadian students at McGill University," he said proudly, "are the great hockey players. In fact the Irish are teaching French Canadians there and at other colleges to play hockey. On this Wanderers team the only French Canadian is the goalie, Ménard. Lester Patrick, a great scorer and passer, the fans call 'The Silver Fox.'

"Did you notice that little guy Ernie Russell? He doesn't weigh more than 140 pounds when he's soaking wet and yet he weaves through with his speed and stick handling. He was the captain of the Montreal A.A. football team."

In the second half the referee brooked no fouls and more than once penalized two members of a seven-man team. The Wanderers seemed lost, all except Ménard the goalie and Patrick the rover, who scored at the ten-minute mark. But the Ottawa goalie Lesueur was frustrating the Wanderers – except when Patrick scored again with three minutes to go. In the last two minutes Ménard made save after save. The Wanderers were skunked 9 to 3 but the total score of the two-game series was 12–10 in favour of the Wanderers, who skated around with the Stanley Cup as Liam and most of the seven thousand spectators cheered.

Celebrating Irish

As Liam was leaving, he offered to take Jack and John Hugh to mass at St. Patrick's Church the next morning and then to show the three men the famous St. Patrick's Day Parade. He told them to be at St. Catherine and St. Urbain at noon. Dress warmly and wear your green scarves, he advised them. John Hugh went back to the hotel and George and Jack went out on the town as usual.

Unable to rouse Jack McDonald the next morning, John Hugh set out to meet Liam for high mass at St. Patrick's Church at the corner of Dorchester and St. Alexander Streets. He took his time and found Liam several minutes before ten o'clock. They sat in a red oak pew halfway up. The green and white streamers still hung from the centre to the pillars, as they had for the Pontifical High Mass on St. Patrick's Day.[5]

Gillis looked at the very high vault of the roof, the stained glass windows and the pulpit with its shamrock and fleur-de-lys pattern. During the service he revelled in the dulcet and diapason tones of the Casavant organ and in the soaring harmony of the choir. In his brief homily, the parish priest, Reverend Father Martin Callaghan, reminded the congregation of the story of Saint Patrick and of their Irish heritage.

View of the nave, St. Patrick's Church

"Irish Celts kidnapped Maewyn Succat, a sixteen-year-old upper-class Briton brought up in the Roman culture, and sold him to a local chieftain as a shepherd slave. His long misery taught him to pray. He escaped to the continent and was ordained as a priest and then as a bishop. Pope Celestine sent him to Ireland because of his fluency in the language. There he established a church near Armagh and converted warrior chiefs and their subjects. He was the first to speak out against slavery and taught love and forgiveness. Fifteen hundred years ago he converted Ireland to Christianity and became known as Saint Patrick. He used the shamrock to explain the idea of the Holy Trinity.

"Today, at this time, we remember our Irish community. Half a million came to Canada before the Great Famine of 1846–52 and many built bridges across the St. Lawrence to Montreal and became the backbone of its industry. Then during the famine many more came. Thousands died of typhus in the transport ships and in quarantine at Grosse Ile. We remember also the Quebec French families who adopted the Irish orphans and let them keep their names. Their response was prompt and open-hearted.

"When we celebrate the parade today, our 82nd in Montreal and the oldest in North America, we pay tribute to the Irish immigrants, to the citizens who saved their children, and especially to the loving and forgiving St. Patrick. Let us commit ourselves as he did in his hymn:

I bind unto myself today
the power of God to hold and lead,
His power to watch, his might to stay,
His ear to hearken to my need;
the wisdom of my God to teach,
His hand to guide, His shield to ward;

the word of God to give me speech,
His heavenly host to be my guard."

George and Jack, looking rather haggard but wearing green scarves as John Hugh was, joined them at noon at St. Catherine and St. Urbain. Despite the snowstorm, many spectators dressed in green lined the route, which began at Atwater. Alderman O'Connell, the grand marshal, rode on a prancing steed at the head of the procession, followed by Alderman Mumbray, who was holding the mighty staff as he represented Mayor Ekers. People cheered the St. Ann's Cadets in their natty uniforms and their drum and fife band. The Ancient Order of Hibernians strode along like proud veterans. Dozens of floats carried patriots and Irish dancers.[6]

After the parade, the three thanked Liam for his many kindnesses and shook his hand. As he left with a cheery wave of the hand, he was aware of the persistent tension and coolness between Gillis and the other two.

Setting Out Alone

At supper John Hugh said a solemn goodbye to George and Jack, who left later in the evening for the high jinks of the Main. Gillis looked at his watch when they rolled noisily in at three in the morning.

The morning of Monday, March 19, they were still sleeping when Gillis had an early breakfast, bade farewell to hotel acquaintances, paid his bill and thanked Madame Bougeant, and went on his way. Eight miles on, he stopped at Lachine for the night. He reached Vaudreuil and Rigaud on ensuing days. At Vankleek Hill he was impressed by the stylish brick buildings of that thriving little town and got a certificate from its mayor. He bought some underwear and socks at the large McLaurin store, which had plate glass counters and electric light. At the Hugh Duncan Drug Store he bought only pencils and stationery, although the store also offered medicines, schoolbooks, silverware and bicycles. He rested his sore feet overnight at Dominion House and talked with its owner, John McLaurin.

The next two days he was at Plantagenet and Leonard, where he rubbed and exercised his feet night and morning. Always he willed himself forward along the railway track. Having gone only 127 miles in eight days, with ever paining feet, John Hugh sometimes thought of giving up but he made no mention of it to the *Ottawa Citizen*, which on March 27 reported his arrival in Ottawa:[1]

ON A WAGER

John Gillis of Sydney Walking
Across the Continent

John H. Gillis, a strapping big descendant of bonnie Scotland, who is walking from Sydney, N.S., to Vancouver, B.C., and return, to win a wager of $1,200, is in Ottawa and has registered at the Grand Union. In order to win the money he must accomplish the remarkable feat inside of a year and a day. He has already covered 1,300 miles and is confident of getting back to the starting and finishing point within the time limited.

Gillis stands about six feet four, is broad-shouldered, long legged and as healthy as the average sailor, and was born in Nova Scotia. The wager was made by a party of his friends.

On March 24[2] the *Sydney Daily Post* had given its front page to a dramatic story with the heading:[2]

PEDESTRIANS PARTED

Social Life in Montreal Proved Too Tempting,
and Some of Them Yielded to Seductiveness

It stated that, according to a letter received, the three walkers had dissolved their partnership and that John Gillis would go on alone. "The rupture, which was pending for some time," took place in Montreal, where "the social world of the big metropolis was too strong an attachment for certain of the trio."

A note four days later on page five announced that Cumming and McDonald were returning home.

The Sydney Record of March 31 carried this item:[3]

CUMMINGS AND McDONALD
TOOK COLD FEET

Gillis, Cummings and McDonald, the three young men who left North Sydney on January 31st to walk across the continent and back, parted company in Montreal last week, Cummings and McDonald abandoning the journey, while Gillis kept on towards 'Frisco. The latter reached Ottawa a few days ago, and was given a letter by the governor-general.

A surprising news item appeared in *The Sydney Record* that same evening:[4]

CUMMINGS AND McDONALD ARE STILL WALKING

Lieut. Harvey McLeod, of the Sydney Field Battery, who returned from the Royal School of Artillery at Kingston, Ont., on Thursday night, reports having come across George Cummings and Jack McDonald, the transcontinental pedestrians, at Kingston last week. The men had walked from Montreal where they had separated from Gillis, who took a different route, to Kingston, and after spending a few hours with Mr. McLeod, started off for Toronto. Mr. McLeod reports both men as being in the best of health and spirits, and it would seem from their talk that they are fully determined to reach 'Frisco within the specified time.

Did George and Jack intend to enjoy the lures of Montreal for a while, then go to Toronto before returning home, as they had told John Hugh? Or had they conspired all along to take the southern route just as soon as the disapproving Gillis was out of the way? Whether they changed their mind or acted as already plotted, they must have moved quickly once Gillis left.

Cumming and McDonald must have left Montreal March 19, the same day Gillis had departed. If so, they covered 223 miles in seven days, a daily average of about thirty-two miles. The *Daily Intelligencer* of Monday, March 26 reported the brief visit of the "Transcontinental Tourists" to Belleville the previous morning.[5]

> Two transcontinental pedestrians, named George Cumming and John McDonald, were in the city for a brief period on Sunday morning ... A third party, whose name could not be learned, started but was forced to give up. Cumming and McDonald are able to subsist by selling lead pencils and some small trinkets which they carry in a small valise. After partaking of breakfast here yesterday morning they proceeded westward.

On arriving in Toronto, George and Jack were almost penniless, having only twenty cents between them. They found and slept in the Salvation Army Barracks[6] where, before bunking down, the men sang hymns to an out-of-tune piano. The next morning, after making themselves more presentable, they got busy telling their story on the street and selling pencils. They raised enough money from interested and sympathetic citizens to buy a square meal, to purchase some needed clothes and to put aside funds for expenses on the next leg of their journey. They were glad to find a pre-Easter sale at the Eaton's department store on Queen Street:[7] wool and merino underwear shirts and drawers, regularly $1.25, for 69 cents each; Scotch tweed trousers, regularly $3.50, for $1.95; a fancy box of dates, 18 cents; a box of Vim cereal, 8 cents.

Spadina Avenue from Queen Street, Toronto

With his charm and wit, George talked himself and his chum into the automobile show, opening that day at the Granite Club Rink, 519 Church Street. Just like many Torontonians, they were mesmerized by the expensive cars that were scaring the horses and threatening to take their place. They admired the Canadian Russell, "the best value in the Show," the English Napier, the Italian F.I.A.T., and the French Clément-Bayard. Among the many American models were names to conjure with: Pierce Arrow, Oldsmobile, Royal Tourist, Stoddard Dayton, Packard, Thomas, Stanley Steamer, Waverly Electric, and a 6-cylinder Ford touring car for $3,200.[8]

On Sunday morning, the first of April, George went to the Richmond Street Wesleyan Methodist Church and Jack attended mass at St. Michael's Cathedral at 200 Church Street. They saw some reminders of the fire that had devastated downtown Toronto just two years earlier on April 19th.

They were sorry to leave this bustling city of a quarter million souls that closed down so quietly and properly on Sundays.

Bay Street after the Toronto fire, 1904

The two men touched base at the *Hamilton Spectator* en route to Chicago via London, Sarnia and Detroit.[9] They arrived in London on Friday, April 5 and at 4:20 p.m. walked into the office of Mr. S. Baker, city clerk, who after a few minutes' conversation signed a certificate of their arrival. A reporter from the *London Free Press* interviewed them, resulting in a long news item the following day about their adventure.[10]

The journalist estimated their age at about twenty-five and recounted the conditions of the wager and the departure from North Sydney on January 31, 1906. They reckoned they had averaged 33 miles a day between Montreal and London (467 miles in 14 days). Once they had managed 43 miles in 10 hours 35 minutes. About financing the trip George Cumming said, "People are pretty generous. We have received as much as $5 for one lead pencil and the lowest price on the average is 25 cents."

Twenty-year-old Jack McDonald did most of the talking this time. Their feet had been "mighty sore" until they got used to walking and they were able to discontinue the use of liniment a month ago. They had not had a sick day since they started.

"We never carry any bundles. Every week we buy clean underclothing[;] and a sweater, pair of knickers and heavy boots and cap are all we wear. Our pipes are great comforts and we couldn't do without them. We plan to follow the track of the Grand Trunk Railway to Chicago and of the Union Pacific to San Francisco."

102

Gillis Hobbles On

In the meantime John Gillis had been making progress, slow-ly at first on account of his painful feet. He found the stretch-es between stations of from fifteen to twenty miles lonesome walking. The station agents welcomed this gangly long-dis-tance walker and provided any assistance they could, but he did not do so well with the section men, most of whom were immigrants from Finland or Italy. By mid-April he had reached Mattawa, on a river of the same name at the Quebec border and just north of the great Laurentian Park. The people of Mattawa were mostly French or Aboriginal but through the parish priest, Gillis was able to find dinner and a bed for the night.

Thus, two and a half months after leaving North Sydney, the three walkers were now broken into two and one. In the month since leaving Montreal, Cumming and McDonald had walked some distance into Michigan and Gillis had reached the place where he would turn west for North Bay and Prince Arthur and trudge across the lonely, rugged lands of the Canadian Shield from Sudbury to Kenora.

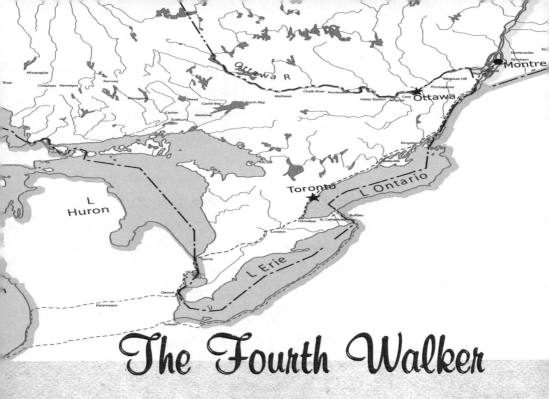

The Fourth Walker

Late Saturday afternoon, April 14, 1906, Charles Henry Jackman said goodbye to friends in Montreal and set out to walk to Vancouver. He was twenty-seven and a former lacrosse player. Having heard about the trek from Cape Breton, he decided to take a long walk "for his health," although his health was not in question. Perhaps he was seeking a peace of mind that would allow him to let go of his glory days playing lacrosse now that his legs would not go fast enough. Could he find the stamina for a greater test?

Jackman must have been planning his journey for some time. He prepared an advertisement to be inserted in newspapers along the way, offering a reward for evidence of his riding on a train or other conveyance. He put in his backpack extra clothes, equipment, a camera and film and got some ready cash for rooms, meals, and repairs and replacement of boots and clothing. He planned to do business as a representative of the

Robert Griig Company of Toronto, the Canadian agents for Pratts Stock Food Company of Philadelphia.

He also bought a little diary (three and a half by six inches) bound in red Morocco leather in which to record his adventure.

Saty, Apl.14/06 Obtained permission from C.P.R. to walk on tracks to Vancouver. Shall always remember the kindness of the chaps in the Vice President's office from whom I obtained much valuable information. Must not forget in particular Hodges, who was responsible for most of it. Met Mr. Lewis of the Star office, who will publish articles should anything out of the ordinary turn up. Hope it may! Said goodbye to the Colonel [Archer] on the roof of the Bath Hotel. Snapped him also. Mr & Mrs De Spargo looked very sorry for me when I bade them adieu. Probably thought I was in for the very deuce of a time. Likely I am. Left for Lachine at 4.30 p.m. Arrived there devilish hungry at 6.30, distance 8 miles. Followed electric car route all the way.

Jackman registered at the Lake View Hotel and enjoyed a "devilish good meal" in the dining room. He spent the evening in the Bath Room pub and went to bed in fine fettle.

Early Days

CHARLES was born August 19, 1878, at Harrogate in North Yorkshire, a town of lovely flowers and elegant spas. He was the second son of Charles Jackman and his second wife, Fanny Silkstone of Shirland, Derbyshire. His father, when still a tailor, had been married to Elizabeth Leyland, a close relative of the Leylands who built bicycles and then automobiles, but Elizabeth had died young. Charles, Sr. eventually became a Prudential Insurance agent and made a home for Fanny, their three children and the daughter of his first marriage. When her husband died, Fanny took in boarders. Kind and optimistic ("she looked out the window, not up the chimney"), she still had to be strict with two towering boys who were always in a tallness competition and who were always clowning around.

Charles said to Jim, "I can fart whenever I want to."

"Go ahead then," retorted Jim.

"But I don't want to," grinned Charles.

"You mustn't use such coarse language, Charles," his mother called from the kitchen. Charles looked and saw her hiding a smile.

Charles grew so fast that the doctor was concerned about his health. This was a time when people dreaded tuberculosis or "galloping consumption." The doctor advised Fanny to take the youth out of school for a while and encourage him to spend time out of doors and to exercise. Charles would be gone for the whole day and sometimes overnight. He carried a backpack containing lunch, dog food and a large water flask as he strode out with a walking stick and their large dog. When he walked west and north he came to the Dales – steeply rolling farmland with dry-stone walls, market towns, ruined castles and abbeys, historic mansions and beautiful gardens, streams and water-falls. After sleeping overnight on the way, he reached the northern frontier of the Dales, walked the ancient Roman roads of Lakeland, climbed the wilderness of Howgill Fells 200 feet high, and saw the waters flowing into the narrow valleys.

When he started east and north from home, he came to vast areas of heather, breathtaking in bloom, interspersed with valleys and woodland. There, too, were historic houses and the ruins of castles and monasteries. The forty-mile day's walk from Osmothersly brought him to Ravenscar, once a Roman signal station, on the coast. Not far then to Whitby with its tall lighthouses, lifeboat station, fishing boats called "Cobbles," and, of course, the ruined abbey and Captain Cook's house in Grape Lane. Outgoing like his mother, Charles talked with and listened to farmers and village people everywhere he went. From that experience he could easily break into the Yorkshire dialect in his story telling.

Glory Days of Lacrosse

Charles played for the Harrogate lacrosse team and worked for the Leyland Company as a bicycle finisher.[1] At the age of nineteen he made the all-star team of North England against South England.[2] The next year his Harrogate team played against Stockport for the North of England championship.[3] Jackman made the all-star team three times and then played two years with Stockport. He was there when Stockport played the touring Canadian team. All the while as an amateur athlete he was earning his living with Leyland, which offered him a position with the firm in India. Instead he took passage to Canada to take up an offer from the Toronto team. He became a works supervisor for McGregor & McIntyre on Pearl Street. An article on page six of *The Toronto Star* on April 4, 1903, introduced him to the public:[4]

> The Toronto Lacrosse Club do not need to worry even if Bert Henry does go back to Brantford. If they want aggressiveness on the home end of the field all they have to do is fill in with Charles Jackman, the big English player who was talked of before Henry came down.
>
> Jackman gave an exhibition of his stamina which should satisfy the most exacting in Pearl Street on Thursday afternoon. Jackman works in a Pearl Street shop. Four rough young fellows dropped around and tried to run matters there for a while. They succeeded until Jackman took a hand in the fun.
>
> Though the other men were armed with shovels, Jackman waded in with his bare hands and cleaned the whole bunch in jig-time. He even brought two of the men into the shop. They escaped while search was being made for a policeman, but Jackman, nothing loth, pursued them up a lane, and after a further encounter with the quartet, came back dragging two of the crowd with him.

When he appeared in the Police Court yesterday to prosecute the men every police inspector in the room cast envious eyes upon the tall, athletic chap in the box, who gave his evidence in such an unostentatious way.

Jackman weighs over two hundred pounds, yet he has not an ounce of superfluous flesh upon his frame. He is a speedy runner, and delights in a hot scrimmage. He played in England with the Stockport team, which has held the English lacrosse championship for eight years in succession.

Jackman and his friend Iler, a former Stockport player, were members of a team that J.J. Cawthra, a Cambridge Blue, assembled to meet the visiting Oxford-Cambridge lacrosse team.[5] Four periods of fifteen minutes were played at Rosedale. In the second the visitors led by 5 to 4 but Cawthra's team won 11 to 9.

During the two seasons that Jackman played for Toronto, his team did well in the Ontario league but usually lost to the powerful Montreal team.

On Easter Sunday, 1906, Charles awoke in Lachine to find the rain pelting down but the weather cleared by half past nine. He took a picture of the hotel and Mr. McRae, the landlord, an "awfully good fellow." He walked along the Lac Saint-Louis road to St. Anne, where he arrived "feeling rather fagged."

Following the Grand Trunk track, he got to the Central Hotel at Vaudreuil in pouring rain. The couple who ran the inn spoke only French. They gave up their room to him with a bed that fit their five-foot height. Being a half-inch short of six feet five inches, Charles found that by putting his foot through the end of the bed he could close the door. "Good night" and "Good morning" were stitched on the pillowcase and pictured angels carrying the message "God bless our home." A man "with a remarkably bad voice" accompanied himself equally badly on an out-of-tune piano. As Jackman wrote in his diary he muttered incantations against the singer. At three in the morning a cat gave such a concert that, beside himself, he fired his revolver at it in the dark!

One has to face it. Charles Jackman's attitude flowed like acid into his diary that Easter Sunday a hundred years ago, in words that would embarrass his family when they read them some time after his death. It was the same superior, arrogant attitude of certain English immigrants at the time that inspired a special note on job signs in some Toronto shop windows. "No Englishman need apply."

Rotten hotel. Grub ditto. French folk running it. Can't speak English. Had to send out for ink. Don't use it here. Presume they use milk instead, thin enough to flow easily ... Shooting very bad — for the cat's proprietor came to me at 7.30 obviously very excited. Gathered from his jabbering that his cat had been shot in the tail. Awfully sad! Poor pussy! Nothing to wag when she's cross ... I therefore understood this five feet of eating humanity to say that the rain had cleared ...

As Jackman walked farther and met people of many ethnic backgrounds he was to experience their sameness, their difference and their kindness: as when French Canadians Mr. and Mrs. Godin deprived themselves and their twelve children in order to give a large meal to a tall, hungry stranger. But at this point, the host of the Vaudreuil hotel was as glad to see the back of Charles Jackman as that ungrateful, prejudiced young Englishman was to leave.

At Lavigne, Charles had a very good and abundant dinner of ham and eggs.

Afterward a young lady who was willing to forsake all and accompany me across the continent. Most interesting. So I snapped her. Her age, as she told me, was five. Got to Rigaud at 3.30 p.m. & met Algernon Sladen. Had tea with him and the pleasure of his company for two miles along the track to St. Eugene. Spent the night there. Distance for the day 28 miles.

At Van Kleek Hill on Tuesday, April 17, Jackman had a lunch of crackers, cheese and soda water. The proprietor charged him twenty-five cents but, on being challenged, itemized the account and settled for twenty cents. A quarter would buy what five dollars does today. Finding that Alfred Station was three miles from Alfred village, Jackman made his way there over an almost impassable road and went to bed fagged out. He took it easy the next morning as "the swarthy daughter of Chene the landlord played and sang at me." Following the road, he reached a dismal hotel in Wendover.

To make Ottawa, he rose up at six on Thursday but driving rain held him indoors four hours. At Rockland he played lacrosse with some boys after lunch and took a picture of Otto Schryer, "who handled his stick very cleverly." He measured height with Albert Ouimet, who beat him by an inch. The weather was unseasonably warm. Charles spent the night at the pretty little village of Cumberlan.

Cumming and McDonald at Kalamazoo

The *Daily News* and the *Evening Chronicle* of Marshall, Michigan, carried an item on Wednesday, April 18 that was copied in the *Battle Creek Enquirer* the next day.[6] It gives the age of John McDonald as nineteen and that of George W. Cumming as twenty-three. The former was actually twenty and the latter thirty-one at the time. Having set forth the place and date of departure and the terms of the wager, the article records their average daily walk as twenty-four and a half miles.

Transcontinental Pedestrians 113

They arrived here from Albion at 5:10 last evening and left for Battle Creek this morning. Yesterday they walked from Jackson to this city. They have letters from the mayors of Detroit, Ypsilanti, Ann Arbor, Jackson and Albion and Mayor Gardanier attached his signature to a letter here.

On April 18, daily newspapers in the United States and Canada carried shocking headlines and narrative about the minute-long earthquake at 5:12 a.m. which wrecked a large part of San Francisco. In the days following, the papers told in words and pictures of the ravaging three-day fire, the loss of life and the human suffering. "Two-thirds of the city destroyed." "Hundreds lie dead beneath the ruins." "300,000 homeless." "Fires still raging." "Thousands face starvation." Then there appeared campaigns across the continent to send relief for the suffering survivors and for the rebuilding of the city.

A reporter for the *Kalamazoo Semi-Weekly Telegraph* interviewed George Cumming and Jack McDonald on Thursday, April 19.[6] George, the spokesman, said they had "averaged a little better than 34 miles a day" since January 31st. "Are we going to win? Of course we are going to win. We are 12 days ahead of our schedule and are getting along splendidly, both financially and otherwise." They showed a letter that Mr. Rush, the town clerk of Kalamazoo, had signed.

But now their goal, San Francisco, the golden city was now in rubble and ashes! How hollow "going to win" sounds in the face of such catastrophe. Furthermore, their average daily walk of thirty-four miles was stretching the truth. Early on, they had lost at least a dozen days on account of very bad win-

114

ter weather and averaged only eighteen or nineteen miles. Only two days before reaching Kalamazoo they reported their average daily walk as twenty-four and a half miles.

Jackman in Ottawa

Charles Jackman arrived in Ottawa at noon on Friday, April 20. He looked up Dick Raby, whom he had last seen in Toronto three years before. They spent the rest of the day in reminiscences. They remembered the game in early April 1899 at the Richmond Athletic Ground near London between the North and the South.[7] "Jackman ran well down, and passed to Heaward, who ran around Taylor, and put the North further ahead ..." "Raby ran down and gave to Smith, who ran around Battersby and scored, and a pass again from Raby to Poole and to A. Mason resulted in a further downfall of the home citadel."[8]

Charles spent the evening at 24 Fourth Avenue with Dick, his wife and their family. He found Mrs. Raby charming "but Halifax English." He had a most enjoyable time and walked two miles to his hotel at two in the morning. On a rainy Saturday he met Dick Raby in his office in the Parliament Buildings. At lunch and during the rest of the day they replayed the games that they had "taken part in in those good old days in Manchester." Charles was not particularly struck with Ottawa. "Like most capitals it seems filled with loafers and seedy hangers on. Particularly clean place. The streets are in fact as well kept as any in Canada."

Feeling better on a beautiful Sunday after a day's rest, Charles followed the road by Britannia Bay and took a photo. Then he walked the Grand Trunk track and spent the night at

Carp. The next day, April 23, he strode ten miles in two hours to Kinburn, with its two stores and The Temperance House, where he had "a jolly good meal." He stopped at Arnprior, a town of four thousand with two sawmills and the headquarters of Sanitaris Table Water. He wrote in his diary:

Very much astonished that I am the man behind Gillis of North Sydney who left there with his brothers early in February to walk to San Francisco and back within a year. Dissatisfied with the other two at Montreal & is now on his own hook & bound for Vancouver. I'd very much like to get ahead of him but he has over three weeks start.

This entry shows how much information Jackman had heard and read about Gillis and the San Francisco project. Although he was wrong about the identity of Gillis's former walking companions, he had everything else right. Trained as an inveterate competitor in lacrosse, he found himself impelled to pass Gillis.

— • —

Charles Jackman did business in Arnprior. He tried to take a photo of the Ottawa River from the track when he discovered that someone, perhaps a chambermaid, had messed with his camera, spoiling the film. The next day he was refused a meal at four houses at Hayley Station but was welcomed most kindly by Rev. P. Pergan and his wife. Charles took a picture of the family and their house.

George Edward Hart

Charles left Pembroke by the Government Road but became confused and did not reach Petawawa until 8:30 at night. He was worn out after a day's trek of forty miles, most of which were without food. At the comfortable McLeans Hotel he met Colonel Aylmer, Lord Aylmer's brother, who was overseeing the construction of the new camp at Petawawa for the professional army. Charles also met Lieutenant Hill, Colonel Aylmer's assistant, a native of Saint Stephen, New Brunswick, and a great friend of Mr. Fraser, with whom Charles had "spent many a jolly evening. On the strength of this we became very chummy." Also in the group at the hotel was a Mr. Westland, a third-year McGill student who had worked on the Grand Trunk Survey during his vacation.

Lieutenant Hill and friend

Jackman roved round the campground with Hill and Westland. He took a snap of them on the way to lunch at the officers' mess. A sociable fellow, Jackman got along with people of all classes and was comfortable with prominent individuals. His interest in people slowed the progress of his walk but he was not committed to a time target. Self-confident but not overbearing, he did not shun the limelight.

Jackman Following Gillis

Arriving at Chalk River, then a small railway town, Jackman found shelter in a very poor hotel. At Mackey he calculated that from Montreal he had walked 203 miles for a daily average of 21 miles.

Sunday, April 29 was hot and the track was poor. Charles dined with Mr. Nesbitt, the section foreman at Aylmer. He groped his way in darkness to Deux Rivières and stumbled into the hotel. "Must avoid walking track at night in the future. Dangerous & very unpleasant. Dangerous from crossing bridges, there is a very good chance of tipping and falling off."

Beastly weather on the last day of April kept Charles Jackman chatting all morning with farmers at the hotel. He then set out on the Government Road through swamp. On the long way he passed only three houses, where Aboriginal women gazed at him with curiosity and many dogs snarled ferociously within a few feet of him. He slogged through several swamps and as he neared Mattawa he saw, but was too tired to appreciate, superb scenery. After a late dinner he relaxed happily with a pile of letters. "I find that Gillis lost much time in this vicinity and is now only 16 days ahead."

The next day Charles had business in Mattawa, a pretty farming and lumbering centre of two thousand people, mostly French and Aboriginals, where Étienne Brûlé had camped in 1610 and Champlain had repaired his canoe five years later. Charles wanted to take pictures of the place but had no film. He lunched at Calvin with the section foreman. At Eau Claire the station agent stamped his book. He found the track rather monotonous and so-so for walking but not as tiring as the average Canadian bush road. With the building of the railways, governments had neglected most roads except those near and within towns and villages. On the railway track he could not get lost and always knew within a sixteenth of a mile how far he was from his destination. John Farmer, the hotel owner in Rutherglen and a keen sportsman, told Charles about hunting the red deer and the scarcer moose and caribou and about fishing trout at Lake Talon, a mile away.

Dredge near North Bay

Waking early Wednesday morning to "disgusting weather," Charles talked with Mr. Farmer until nine. Although the rain had stopped, the sky was dark and threatening. He decided to take a chance but twenty minutes on his way the rain pelted in torrents. To save a mile, he followed the muddy road and then, ruing his failure to learn from experience, returned to the railway track at Bonfield. He finished his extremely wet walk at North Bay.

Deceiving Duo

On May 2 *The Daily Standard* of St. Catharines[1] announced
"The city this morning was treated to a visit by two gentlemen
who are now on the home stretch of an eight thousand mile
tramp. They are John McDonald and George W. Cummings, of
North Sydney, C.B., and while the men have that travel-stained
appearance they nevertheless possess a gentlemanly spirit
beneath their worn and shabby clothing."

"Home stretch"? "Gentlemanly spirit"? Not quite. The inter-
viewer reported that the men left their native Sydney on July
31, 1905 (six months earlier than their actual departure) and
that "[f]rom Chicago they completed the journey via the Union
Pacific and arrived on January 29th at 'Frisco. After a stay of
two days they recommenced their tramp, travelling via Chicago
and Buffalo to the Falls." The article goes on to say that they
were several days ahead of time and that John McDonald had
worn out six pairs of shoes and gained ten pounds. They paid

TWO PECULIAR VISITORS; ARRIVE IN THE CITY.

The city this morning was treated to a visit by two gentlemen who are now on the home stretch of an eight thousand mile tramp. They are John McDonald and George W. Cummings, of North Sydney, C.B., and while the men have that travel-stained appearance they nevertheless possess a gentlemanly spirit beneath their worn and shabby clothing.

It was on July 31st, 1905, on the way but were to sell pencils and to return to Sydney with $200.

The trip to San Francisco was duly made. They walked the ties of the I.C.R. and C.P.R. from St. John's, N.B., to Sherbrooke, and the G.T.R. to Chicago. From Chicago they completed the journey via the Union Pacific and arrived on January 29th at 'Frisco.

After a stay of two days they recommenced their tramp, travelling via Chicago and Buffalo to the Falls.

They are now several days ahead of time, having been given one year and one day to make the journey. Mr. McDonald gained ten pounds and so far has worn out six pairs of shoes.

The men have the mayors of the various municipalities through which they pass sign a book carried by a visit to Mr. Riddell, the mayor of St. Catharines, to get his signature in their book.

Was this Baron Munchhausen and his aide, talking to a reporter? What were Cumming and McDonald thinking of? Certainly not their good names! There was a time they might have got away with such a fairy tale – before the invention of the telephone and the telegraph. What was the truth behind all this hot air?

They might have walked the 144 miles from Kalamazoo to Chicago in three days and a fraction, for they left Kalamazoo in the afternoon of April 19. At best they would have reached Chicago on April 22 but more likely on April 23. The big-city newspapers did not record the trivia of the arrival in Chicago of the cross-continent walkers, especially when many of their pages were filled with news and pictures of a devastated San Francisco.

Two events probably influenced the two men to turn back. Not only had the San Francisco catastrophe sunk into their consciousness but they had the misfortune, they said, to be robbed by hoboes.

If they left Chicago the next day, they travelled 570 miles in seven or eight days in order to be in St. Catharines the morning of May 2. If, however, they left Kalamazoo on April 20 and went directly to St. Catharines, via Toledo and Buffalo, they had twelve days to walk 480 miles. In either case, given the distances and their shortage of money, they must have had help from a railway freight car moving in that direction.

A dispatch from St. Catharines to the *Sydney Daily Post* reported that Cumming and McDonald were there with only ten cents in their pockets.[2] The *Post* item gave January 31, 1906, as the date of their departure from North Sydney and stated that they "were fourteen days ahead of their schedule." Indeed, they had "averaged 32 miles a day."

Gillis Makes Good Time

The first day of May at Wayland, 202 miles west of Sudbury, Gillis was ensconced in a hotel and writing a letter to the Sporting editor of the *Sydney Daily Post*. That paper gave him the headline:[3]

ST. JOSEPH'S LONE PEDESTRIAN

*Keeps Heading Toward the West
and Expects to "Get There"*

John Hugh was relieved to boast that after departing from Sudbury he had averaged thirty-four miles a day, "a pretty good walk for six consecutive days on a railroad track in a hot sun," especially as the stretches between stations were "pretty lonesome travelling." At Chapleau, a miserable fellow stole his photographic plate. Friendly men "went in search of the thief, and had they found him, he would have fared badly at their hands." The weather was very warm during the day but after sunset it turned cold. Gillis promised to write again when he arrived in Port Arthur around the 14th or 15th.

Jackman Aims for Sudbury

On May 1 Jackman reached Rutherglen, just about three hundred miles from Wayland, where Gillis was writing his letter. At that rate, by walking a few more miles than Gillis each day, Jackman might catch up to him. Although he doesn't harp on it in his diary, Jackman kept it in the back of his mind. He was getting so close that sooner or later he would pass the Cape Bretoner in a walking race (as he saw it) for Vancouver.

F.P. Brady, the general superintendent of the Lake Superior Division of the Canadian Pacific Railway, "awfully nice chap," gave Charles Jackman a permit to walk the track to Fort William. Charles had his shoes half-soled and fitted with new heels. He wrote a letter to the *Daily Times Journal* of Fort William[4] in which he mentioned it and stated that his shoes were well made, had a sole three-quarters of an inch thick, and were well spiked to prevent slipping. Intending to beat all walking records between North Bay and Sturgeon Falls, Charles walked the first ten miles in two hours. Then he twisted his ankle. His progress was now so painful that he took two hours to cover the four miles to Meadowvale, where he hoped to find a bed at Section F but instead had to be satisfied with a short rest and a meal of eggs. At half past eight in the evening he set out for Sturgeon Falls and limped the ten miles through cool, very windy weather in three hours. At nearly midnight he was happy to find an open restaurant, where he relished ham and eggs.

"Like a giant refreshed," he awoke Friday, May 4 and discovered that his ankle was almost better. During the morning he rested and took two snapshots of the turbulent rapids where the Sturgeon River runs into Lake Nipissing. At this logging centre, once a fur trading post of the Hudson's Bay

Sturgeon Falls

Company, he learned that there was great fishing for bass, muskie, pike, whitefish and walleye. He spent an hour at McFarland's Store at Cache Bay and, troubled only a little by his sprained ankle, settled in a clean, comfortable hotel in Verner, a largely French lumbering and farming village with two hotels and four stores.

Feeling fit Saturday morning but with a strong, cold wind dead in his teeth, Charles plodded to Markstay, where he registered at the one "indifferent" hotel, "the grub in particular being very much off." He picked up a *Toronto Daily Star* from May 4 containing his account of his tramp from Montreal to North Bay.[5] It reproduced a letter dated May 2 "from Charles Henry Jackman, the ex-Toronto lacrosse player, more recently of Halifax. He reported that he had covered 386 miles in eighteen days, two of which he had spent in Ottawa. His walking average was about twenty-four miles a day.

I leave here to-morrow for Sturgeon Falls, spend Sunday in Sudbury, and expect to reach Port Arthur before the end of the month. It promises to be a most uninteresting month, for the country between Sudbury and Port Arthur is very sparsely settled. Nothing out of the ordinary has occurred so far. Am very fit and hard as nails and, barring accidents, shall reach Vancouver four months from date of starting...

The snowy, cold Sunday made for a "beastly walk" to Wahnapitae, a rough lumbering town. From there, Charles trudged soggily through the rain into the comfortable New American Hotel in Sudbury. The next day was so cold that he took the day off and spent much of it "talking with that very good sort, D.L. MacKinnon." He learned about the new methods invented six years ago for refining nickel, which led to its use in making armoured steel for warships. That put Sudbury on the map.

Making It Up as they Go Along

In Toronto, Cumming and McDonald repeated their fabrications about leaving Cape Breton in July of 1905 and walking all the way to San Francisco and back to Ontario. A front-page story in *The Toronto Daily Star* on Saturday, May 5, laid it all out:[6]

Two jolly wager tramps, George Cummings and John McDonald of Sydney, Cape Breton, spent last night in Toronto in the course of their eight thousand mile tramp from their home to San Francisco and back, on a $1,200 bet. They are now on their way home. The two men are bronzed with the suns of half a dozen States and Provinces, but their robust constitutions do not appear to have deteriorated in vigor or capacity as the result of their long trip on shank's mare.

They left Cape Breton in July, 1905, and passed through Toronto on their way last fall ... They have yet to travel 1,235 miles, and are confident they can do it, and earn the $1,200. In their school bags, in which they carry all their spare belongings, they have signed certificates of entry from reputable citizens of all the towns they went through. Their route was via Sarnia, Detroit, Chicago, Omaha and the Union Pacific Railroad (Pullman ties) to 'Frisco.

They earned their subsistence selling lead pencils and doing odd jobs towards the requisite $400 cash. They spent the morning selecting new knickerbockers, jumpers and boots in which to continue the rest of their journey. Their old clothes were practically worn out.

128

What is more, they had already found the time to earn $200 dollars each doing odd jobs, half a year's wages for unskilled workers. Perhaps George sang for a living and John gave gymnastic exhibitions. The signed certificates they claimed to have were surely forged. Did they expect to get away with it? In those new days of telegraph and telephone and of newspapers that watched and quoted one another, were George Cumming and Jack McDonald so ignorant and naïve as to believe that they could gull trusting reporters or readers for long? Were they having sick fun with a reporter who thought he was dealing with reasonably truthful men?

The fun didn't last long. Four days later the *Sydney Daily Post*, front page, was reprinting an article from *The Toronto Daily Star*[7] with a new headline:

SLIGHTLY INACCURATE

Have the Cape Breton Pedestrians Been Pulling Newspaperman's Leg

The Post also reprinted an article[8] from the *Toronto Mail and Empire* with the heading PEDESTRIANS FAKING. The truth was out. "Their memories must have failed them in the journey" said the *Mail and Empire*, for they "were in Toronto only six weeks ago. They had an entirely different set of dates with them last week. On their first appearance here March 26, they claimed to have left home on New Year's Eve, but last week announced that they started from Sydney on the 31st of last July."

Tracking Through Wilderness

Charles Jackman said goodbye Tuesday mid-morning to his Sudbury friends, who gave him "provisions galore." He trekked in the cold and picnicked near Cartier in the bush covered with snow. The next day he took it easy until late in the morning and then had a picnic lunch in the bush of Grapenuts, crackers, sardines and beef tea, which he thought was a strange mixture indeed. At Strolak he had afternoon tea with the station agent, "an awfully nice little Englishman named Fulcher." The CPR track was taking him into a vast wild country of forest, rock, lakes and rivers. He stopped at Pogamasing, where he met the Soules, father and son, who kept comfortable bachelor quarters. Charles enjoyed the evening and found the old man most interesting; he bunked on the floor.

Pogamasing looked so pretty Thursday morning, May 10 that Charles took a snap of the station with precipitous cliffs behind it and the Spanish River in front. Someone told him that old Mr. Soules ate venison every day. Charles stopped at the station house in Metagama, where the French night operator and his wife lived with more than a dozen children. When she cooked a large dish of ham and six eggs, she said it was just for him. Thanking this generous couple, he went on to Biscotasing, where there was no bed available for him. A boarding-house couch "big enough for a jack rabbit" kept him sleepless all night after a long walk. He was so tired the next morning that he "refused to photograph the pretty town." A good large lunch at the Ramsey section house reduced his weariness and he strode on to Woman River, where the section foreman gave him comfortable quarters and an enjoyable night.

A good sleep and a long rain led to a relaxed morning with the station agent. In fact, Charles cooked the fried eggs for the noon meal. He took his time walking to Ridout, where Mr. Inman, the section foreman, welcomed him. Although Mrs. Inman took ninety minutes getting the supper ready, she proved herself a good cook.

On Sunday Charles walked to Nemegosis, where he lunched with Mr. Hatch, the operator, "a really first rate chap," and so enjoyed the company of Mr. and Mrs. Hatch that he accepted an invitation to stay the night. He took a picture of them and their child and went to sleep in a very cozy bedroom.

At Chapleau the next day Charles met Jim Jackman of Lauger and Jackman, general merchants – "decent little chap but somewhat fussy." He enjoyed talking with the day operator and the postmaster. The latter loaded him down with cigars and the former invited him to comfortable quarters. He learned that Chapleau had begun as a CPR town and also became a lumbering centre with lots of wildlife and a largely French and Aboriginal culture.

Here and in many other centres Charles Jackman was taking orders for livestock feed at general stores, large stables and implement stores. He sent orders back by post or telegram and from time to time received money from the company by wire, sometimes rather late. Thus he was financing his walk, which had to fit in with his business calls.

Leaving in the pouring rain, Charles walked until four o'clock, when the sun came out and so warmed the day that he enjoyed a dip in a lovely little lake. The "just ripping" scenery made him sorry that he had run out of film and had shipped his camera to Fort William. He walked along a chain of pretty lakes and often spotted deer in the distance. In good fettle he arrived in Wayland and had "a rattling good supper with J. Godin, who is blest with a wife who knows how to cook." Upton, the operator, generously lent his quarters to Charles and went to Chapleau to sleep. The Godins gave the wayfarer a good breakfast, "Must try to remember this & endeavour to make some small return." They sent him away with an immense lunch, which he later enjoyed beside a brook. Before that, because the day was extremely hot, he swam in a lake that he had all to himself. A long, strenuous walk in the heat brought him wearily to Missanabie.

Thursday May 17/06. Left Missanabie 8 a.m. Had lunch in the bush and wasted considerable time cooling myself in a little lake. If anything, warmer than yesterday. Still had 20 miles to go at 5 p.m. & it felt confoundedly like a shower, the air being very oppressive. The storm broke when I was still 8 miles from Grassett. Time 8.30. Just the worst I ever *experienced, for in addition to the thunder and lightning, hailstones hacked me very unkindly. Landed at Grassett 10.30 completely exhausted. Met with much kindness at the hands of Mr Reynolds the agent, who gave me a jolly good supper & a bed for the night. Dis. for day 35 miles.*

The next morning Charles reluctantly left the "noble old chap" Mr. Reynolds and came at last to White River, where he found a comfortable little hotel with excellent food. He took Saturday off because he badly needed repairs, especially to his boots. He spent the day indulging in strongman feats with the men of White River.

Devilish lonely walk & at 9.30 it became so dark one could scarce find one's way over the track. Glorious Northern Lights made things a little better however later & enabled me to see a bear shambling towards the bush. I didn't follow. My legs in fact seemed to hurriedly acquire an uncontrollable desire to go as speedily in the opposite direction. It became very dark again at 10.30 & I almost fell off the very high bridge that one has to cross to get to Heron Bay. A train was approaching & I started to run. At the first stride I tripped & went sprawling almost into the water 100 feet below. Picked myself up & just got across in time to avoid the train. Must avoid walking after nightfall in future. Too risky!

Charles reached Heron Bay thirty minutes before midnight, thus ending a historic daily trek of fifty-six miles. Everyone was asleep except the night operator, Mr. Dowd, who gave him the key to his rather diminutive cottage, telling him to make himself at home. In these seemingly palatial quarters the hiker made himself a meal and laid down his weary bones most gratefully. Mr. Dowd appeared for breakfast. Charles spent the morning with him and the local CPR agent, at whose house he had a good lunch. Before he had gone far on his "monotonous grind" he met the roadmaster of White River and talked with him for ten minutes, thus giving "his horny handed bunch" a respite.

He got to Coldwell, found comfortable quarters with Mr. Chisholm, the agent, and talked with him and the night operator, Mr. Hawke, "Toronto-born and a jolly good sort." Charles had met Chisholm's brother several times in Antigonish, Nova Scotia. Astonished to see a piano, Jackman entertained "the good people of Coldwell by wading through his "extensive repertoire." He was not a musician but was musical enough to clown on the piano.

So wet was the morning of Tuesday, May 22 that Jackman took time off to do a little rifle practice with Hawke. He left immediately when the weather cleared at eleven. He had dinner with a three-hundred-pound man, A.A. Baldwin, the agent at Middleton, "a very good sort." His wife's cooking was superlative.

Angry Gillis in Port Arthur

John Hugh Gillis, in Port Arthur May 22, wrote a letter[1] to the *Sydney Daily Post* in reply to material that had been printed in that paper from the diary of his former companions. He felt he had been placed in a wrong light. The events of the trip as far as Montreal were correct but much of it was "not consistent with the great principle" (whatever that was, perhaps the Golden Rule). He avoided naming the writer of the diary. "Suffice to say his cranium is rather devoid of hirsute appendages for a man of his youth. His greatest defect, however, is a lack of veracity in much of what he is wont to say, and those who are acquainted with him know that he is wont to say a little more than the average man." Gillis continued:

> He makes several allusions to my "throwing the Gaelic." I am proud to be able to say that I can speak that language and I do not know any man with Scotch blood in his veins but who is not or would not be proud if he could speak it – with the exception of the person who in writing his diary would lead one to believe that speaking Gaelic, or "throwing it," as he vulgarly puts it, was not exactly the thing to do ... Being a Scotchman himself, and not possessed of the accomplishment of speaking that glorious old tongue, he considers it vulgar in another man to be able to speak it.
>
> There are other nasty allusions in that "diary" that should be corrected but "murder will out," and I will leave the public to judge for themselves. Since leaving Montreal, although travelling alone

and through a great deal of desolate country, I cer-
tainly feel it preferable to travelling in company
with the others. Their actions and conduct, partic-
ularly in Montreal, made it compulsory on my part
to cover the long journey alone. This step met with
the approval of the promoter of the scheme, who
decided that I should make Vancouver, via the
C.P.R. main line, my objective point on the Pacific
coast, instead of San Francisco.

My health is in excellent condition, and my
feet, which caused me to lose so much time at first,
are as well as ever they were, so I have good
hopes of getting back to North Sydney in the time
allotted, and I expect to bring back absolute proof
that I have walked the whole distance going both
ways.

May 23, Jackman Forges Ahead

Charles had gone less than five miles when he passed the conductor Henry McCuagh, a pleasant chap whom he had often
seen between White River and Jackfish. McCuagh threw him a
huge bag of bananas and oranges. The sociable hiker had
lunch with Mr. Brown of the CPR Telegraph Department, who
was laying the wire between White River and Schreiber for the
Montreal-Winnipeg connection. Those men had their own
boarding car and were living well. Reaching Schreiber, situated in a pretty highland valley, Jackman went immediately to
the barber and then spent the evening with the agent and the
operator, "both first raters."

Rossport, looking south to islands on Lake Superior, a great place for fishing and hunting, was Charles's next stop. At the excellent hotel, which served a good lunch, he was pleased to meet the owner, Mr. Spencer, a Manchester man who had long operated a cotton business in England. Mrs. Spencer, "a kind-hearted old soul," spoke with a strong accent. Having spent three hours with them, Charles set out for Gravel. He had supper at the cottage of the section foreman and then found comfortable quarters with the agent. The weather was so bad on Friday that Charles spent a long time looking at the Williston collection of many and varied photographs. Some were of the lazy, meandering Gravel River with a bird's-foot delta where it flowed into Lake Superior.

Determined to make up for a slack day, Charles strode to Kama, where he had lunch in a boarding car with the conductor of the work train. He hurried across the long bridge over the Nipigon River and walked the CPR track right into the business core of Nipigon. He learned about the fur trading post of long, long ago, about fish to be caught and animals to be hunted, about logging and about mining marble, sandstone and gravel.

As Nipigon was not far enough for him that day, Charles walked four hours to Wolf, fifty miles from his morning's starting point but at nearly half-past ten everybody was in bed. In vain he tried to wake the agent. After he had wandered around he saw a light in the bush and groped his way some distance. In a rude camp sat a Lancashire man who was "out of cash and almost out of food." With true Lancashire hospitality, the camper offered the lone hiker enjoyable pancakes and fried ribs. Charles tried to fit his long frame into a soapbox-like bunk but gave up and wandered around until, at seven, he "came across a bridge gang in a boarding car just about to sit down to a breakfast of porridge and eggs and bacon."

At Pearl, Charles had Sunday lunch with the operator and his wife, a jolly, carefree little woman from Halifax, whose company he enjoyed so much that he didn't get away until mid-afternoon. At MacKenzie he had "tea" with the section foreman, a very unattractive personality. For the poor supper his host asked fifty cents and Jackman gave him a quarter. But, as darkness fell, he would have liked to stay there for the night.

Didn't like the look of Mr. Section Man however, so started out on a 14 mile tramp in the dark. Very lonely and unpleasant it was too. The track seemed to be a mass of line stakes & I tripped & sprawled many times. The line runs through the bush all the way to Port Arthur, at which place I arrived fagged out at midnight. Sought out a restaurant on arrival and had a big feed. Put up at the Algoma Hotel for the night after covering 50 miles. That completed 100 miles in two days & 1000 miles from Montreal.

M⁹ˢ G[Spencer] is a kind hearted old soul. with an accent that smacks of an "Owdham" flavor

Left Rosepark. 5.6ᵃ
arrived Oxford. 9.8ᵃ

The ag⁹ was out but I managed to get a very good tea at the Retion Foreman Cottage (Audelon)

Got very comfortable Quarters with Williston on his return.

Dis. covered 30 miles

Friday may 25.

Beastly day: Slacked.
Williston is a keen photographer + we spent the afternoon reading through various prints + negatives of which he has a vast + interesting Collection

A two-page spread from the Jackman diary.

53

Saty. May 26/06

Said Good bye to my friends
Williston + J. Reid. (Campers)
at. 8.15. a m.
                    Had lunch
at Kama (16 miles) on a
boarding Car with Mr
Bartlett. Conductor work train
they left me behind at Kama
and I very much astonished
them by Catching up
to them 5½ miles west
of there an hour afterwards
Arrived Nepigon 5 p m.
(33 miles) Left Nepigon
6.30 arriving Wolf.
(50 miles) at. 10. 20. p m
to find that few mortals
lie there in bed
                    I endeavoured
to waken R. O'Neil the
agt but without success.
After wandering around
for some time I spied a
light some distance away
in the bush. Made for it
found it occupied by a

When Jackman arrived in Fort William there was great excitement in the town. At lunch he read black headlines on the front page of the *Daily Times Journal*[2] of Monday, May 28, 1906:

OGILVIE ELEVATOR A COMPLETE WRECK

Huge Grain Handling Plant Shifted from Its

Foundation into the Kaministikwia River

Contained 380,000 Bushels of Wheat Most

of Which Will Be Saved — Loss Exceeds $500,000

— Work of Clearing Underway

Charles wrote a paragraph in his diary about the drastic accident, stating that 150 men were busy shovelling the wheat into bags and that he had taken two snapshots of the wreck. He did business on Tuesday in the town, including getting a permit to walk the CPR track to Winnipeg. He spent the evening with correspondence. Because the weather was so bad on Wednesday he had time to learn about the twin towns of Port Arthur[3] and Fort William. "They are both go-ahead places, each with a population of 11,000 & great rivalry exists between the two."

— • —

Thursday, the last day of May, Charles gave up his miserable walking in the drizzling rain at Kiministikwia, where he met two men, Nesbitt and Simple, who were trying to get original photos of the district: "very likeable chaps & well travelled." "Simple loves his name, for in earnest he may resemble a fox."

Charles was now following a railway track that had been

142

Above: Elevator collapse. Below: Elevator down

hacked from Finmark to Dryden, Kenora, and the Manitoba border through a region of innumerable lakes and rivers, valleys, rocky heights and forests and of isolated hamlets to serve the railway and harvest the natural resources.

The first of June, a Friday, Jackman had supper at a Grand Trunk camp a mile east of Oeno, and finished at Dexter, where he met the night operator, "a very good Irishman from Limerick."

The next day in Savane he tried without success to get a meal. The agent was dirty and unobliging. The mistress of the Finland Boarding House shut the door in his face. Hunger forced him to open the door and follow her to the kitchen, whereupon she scuttled to the back yard, slamming the door behind her. He took some cookies, drank some milk and left ten cents on the table. He failed to imagine what it was to be a woman suddenly confronted by a gigantic tramp. He had a good supper at the section house in Biotin and after a day's thirty-six miles strolled quite fresh into Carlstadt at 9:30.

The night operator there proved to be a very wooden headed young man about as lively as a dead tortoise. The best obtainable was a bed in a room that contained another bed occupied by two Finlanders. Very uninviting sort of place & stuffy as the deuce. Opened the window & with the fresh air came an army of mosquitoes ... The mosquitoes bit me so badly I couldn't sleep a wink. Got up at 3 a.m. & smoked furiously. The mosquitoes in this country are quite fond of tobacco & it only induced them to come from other quarters.

George and Jack Mesmerize Montreal

The *Montreal Star* of Saturday, June 2, 1906, carried a long article on its front page:[4]

THOSE FAST WALKERS MAKING A RECORD

Sunburnt, dust-begrimed, and weather beaten, wearing green figured sweaters, straw hats and knickerbockers, with leather bags and crooked canes as their impedimenta, there arrived in Montreal this morning George W. Cummings and John McDonald, the two pedestrians who started from North Sydney, N.S., in the beginning of last October to walk to San Francisco and back in 365 days, for the stake of $1200.

To accomplish this feat of travelling 8,000 miles it was necessary that they should travel an average of twenty-two miles a day. They claim to have actually averaged thirty-eight miles and this time they intend to put in a visit to Great Britain where they think they will be able to walk from Glasgow to Land's End and be back to Montreal in time to walk the remainder of the distance to Cape Breton by the 18th of October, when the year expires.

They claim to have loyally adhered to the terms of their contract. They left North

Sydney without a cent, and have neither begged, borrowed or stolen.

They were entertained at lunch today by the proprietors of the Grand Trunk restaurant at Bonaventure, and during the morning they recited their adventures to various small groups of admirers. They claim to have maintained themselves by the sale of pencils, pictures and small articles of stationery. They say they have passed through a series of adventures more or less of a sensational character, which they intend to publish in book form.

They bring with them letters from the town clerks of the principal cities they have visited, and show a note book stamped with the names of station agents of the railway along whose tracks they have walked, purporting to certify that they have never ridden by train.

The whole of their walking has been over railway tracks. They say they were once robbed of their possessions by hoboes ...

The *Moncton Transcript* carried a brief item[5] that claimed because Cumming and McDonald "were two months ahead of their schedule, they decided to take a side trip to England, and sailed from Montreal on Friday. They will visit London, Glasgow and Dublin, and are due to arrive in North Sydney Christmas Day."

The *Sydney Daily Post* reprinted this squib[6] with the headline, "Another Pipe Dream."

Jackman Walks Toward History

Sunday morning, June 3, the rain came down in torrents. After a lunch of bread and butter and cocoa with the agent, Charles left Carlstadt at two, disgusted with the place. At English River he met the night operator, "an extremely nice fellow," and the Grand Trunk engineer, who found Charles a bunk in the camp. The next day Jackman got to Bonheur in time to escape a storm.

The Overtaking

June 5, 1906, turned out to be a historic day in the young life of Charles Jackman. Overnight, mosquitoes had raised huge blisters over his body and especially on his painful ankles. He found the railway agent at Bonheur conceited and repulsive.

As the guest of the boarding car cook, Charles ate a good breakfast and found another boarding car with good cooks at lunchtime in Falcon. He wrote three pages in his small diary about the operation of the boarding car system. One man owned the system from North Bay to Fort William and another man from there to Winnipeg. They always had good cooks and "cookees." Unless the food was plentiful and well cooked the gangs would leave the job, as did 125 men not far from Falcon. Cooking was on a wholesale scale: fifty slices of bacon cooked on a three-foot frying pan and tea boiled in a miniature water tank. At Falcon the work gang was so big that the cook had three helpers. Charles ate after the gang left. Then he walked by mid-afternoon to Ignace on Agimak Lake and enjoyed the beauty of the northern landscape.

Boarding car at Bowfield, Ontario

A little farther on, at Butler on Raleigh Lake, the former lacrosse player and lone walker forgot the misery of his sleep-less night, and the blisters of his mosquito bites, to greet another lone hiker, an athlete his equal in height but five years younger, who earlier had walked slowly and rested often to overcome his foot trouble but was now in good walking shape.

"I'm Charles Jackman," he introduced himself. "I've been trying to catch up to you. To tell you the truth, I thought of passing you, but now, having walked 1,200 miles alone, I'd be glad of your company if you don't mind."

"Then I guess you know I'm John Gillis from North Sydney," the other replied. "I heard you were behind me since Montreal and shortening the distance between us. I had trouble with my feet for a while and that slowed me down. Although I made friends at various stops, I did find the walking lonesome and would be glad to share the long stretch ahead with you."

They eyed each other and noted that they were of the same height. "I guess we'll be able to keep in step," said Jackman.

"Every step of the next 1,800 miles," Gillis laughed, as they strode off together.

— • —

Two friendly, outgoing men, they had so much to say to each other and they would have lots of time to say it. They talked about the recent experiences of their lonely trek as they walked until daybreak to Taché. That night in his diary Charles wrote about "Gillis of North Sydney, who is walking to the coast & back within a year and who was one month ahead of me at Ottawa. He is 6 ft 4 tall, of thin but athletic build & quite good looking. He is working his way through by selling cards with his photograph on."

The map shows locations including L Manitoba, Selkirk, Beauséjour, Whitemouth, Poplar Point, Rosser, Winnipeg, Portage La Praire, Virden, Oak Lake, Brandon, and the Red R.

Tramping Westward

At Taché an American by the name of Friend did not belie his name, for he gave the tall hikers some biscuits to allay their hunger. No beds were available at the boarding house, so Jackman smoked his pipe until breakfast while Gillis tried fitfully to get some sleep on a bench. His arm was under his head for a pillow and his legs dangled over the end. Finally he twisted his gangling frame and sat up. His arm felt like pins and needles.

"Hello, did you get any sleep sitting in that chair?"

"I didn't think it was worth the trouble. I just puffed on my pipe. It's getting rather rank so I'll have to clean it. Do you feel refreshed?"

"I ache all over but I guess I nodded off. Can't say I feel refreshed."

The two travellers ate a solid breakfast of porridge, ham and eggs, toast and hot tea, which made up somewhat for the bad night. As they left, the boarding house mistress carefully eyed them to make sure they hadn't made off with any of her belongings.

Arriving at Brule at 11:30 a.m. we endeavoured to get lunch at a section house. The Finnish woman who lived there was very much afraid of us gigantic tramps. Gillis tried in vain to make her understand what we wanted while I sat & laughed at his almost futile effort. I say almost futile, for he did manage to get six eggs & a loaf of bread through a half open window for the sum of one quarter. This we took to a nearby hut & started a fire, in an old stove. While Gillis was busy with the fire I tried my luck at the house & succeeded rather brilliantly, for I managed to get some tea, a teapot & a frying pan, butter & all sorts of good things. These I carted over to the hut & we managed rather well after all. I got all these for nothing too.

They strolled on to Dinorwic after lunch and then, crossing the river bridge, came to Wabigoon for supper. Each of these places, they discovered, was situated on a lake of the same name. Three miles on, a threatening storm "broke with awful fury." Finding little shelter in the bush, they decided to retreat back to Wabigoon, where they arrived like drowned chipmunks at half past nine. The men were forced to pass the next day, Thursday, June 7, in Wabigoon on account of the bad weather. They met a retired army officer, Captain Johnson, owner of the Webster and Marlow Steamship Company, and spent a pleasant night in the handsome little home of that most interesting man, "every inch a soldier."

Jack McDonald in Quebec City

Around the time Gillis and Jackman were in Wabigoon, Jack McDonald visited the office of the *Quebec Chronicle* and told a whopper that had grown even taller since the week before. He regaled the reporter with the tale that he was finishing a tramp of eight thousand miles he and a companion had begun eight months ago. Citing the conditions of the wager, he stated that, once home, they would receive $1,200 each. The news item was reported as follows:

> Both have been to San Francisco and are now on their way back to Sydney. At Sherbrooke they separated, McDonald coming to Quebec, while his companion will follow the railway track down to Halifax. They have yet four months to complete the journey but McDonald expects to be able to cover the distance in five weeks. In passing through cities and towns, the trampers are compelled to get certificates from the mayors and city clerks. McDonald exhibited several documents showing the places he had passed through. He is in good health and spirits, although he says sometimes he suffered hardship. On one occasion he and his companion walked

forty miles without getting anything to eat. They usually walked four miles an hour or forty-eight miles in a day of 12 hours. McDonald visited the city hall yesterday to get a certificate from his worship the mayor or the city clerk. He will continue his journey this morning to Sydney.

The *Sydney Daily Post* reprinted the story[1] with new headlines: Still Stringing Them: Fakers "Take in" Easy Westerners – Bluff Not Yet Called.

Dryden and Kenora

Gillis and Jackman walked the morning of June 8 through forest and over rolling terrain to Dryden, a pretty place on Wabigoon Lake. They registered at a comfortable hotel on the corner of Earl and Duke Streets. It was owned by Andrew Hutchison, "a particularly nice chap," who was properly proud of his ten-year-old hospice, Dryden's first. Dryden itself, a successful little town, was founded by the Hon. John Dryden, as a large "Pioneer Farm" in 1894. The very next year survey crews cleared trail for the Canadian Pacific Railway and, after that, workers strung telegraph line from Thunder Bay to Winnipeg. Dryden also boasted a board and paper mill driven by waterpower. Gillis and Jackman retired to their beds by lamplight, even as the first telephones in Dryden were getting a workout and men were busy with construction and supplies for Swan Swanson, who had a contract for a section of the Grand Trunk Railway.

The two hikers were delayed when Charles discovered he had left his knapsack in Ignace, and it had to be sent on to Dryden. John busied himself selling souvenir cards.

Once again, the men could not find beds for the night. Station house benches were not the best places for restful sleep. On Sunday morning they stopped at a no vacancy boarding house for breakfast. And what a disgusting meal it was: the porridge was lumpy and barely warm, the toast was limp and soggy, the eggs half cooked and the tea a weak slop. "We should have taken the cook's name," Jackman said.

On that very hot day both men suffered great thirst. There was no available water to drink. With lips parched, tongues swollen and throats sore, neither talked much. Charles mumbled to his partner, "I'm sorry, Gillis, you're having such an unusually hard time without Adam's ale." John Hugh was initially offended but caught the joke, and laughed.

"I suppose that makes up for your painful reaction to mosquitoes and black flies while I enjoy the resistance I built up from my childhood. I remember going fishing at the mill dam early one Saturday morning with Rod, my first cousin. The black flies settled on me but they didn't hurt, so I didn't brush them off. Sunday morning I was putting on my starched collar for the choir and looked in the mirror. My eyes were slits and my whole face looked like a pumpkin. Needless to say, I didn't show my face at mass that day."

Both were cheered by a good noontime dinner of roast beef, potatoes and gravy and rice pudding with raisins at a boarding car. Then they took it easy until mid-afternoon.

Arrived at Parson's Camp at 5.30 & met the Rev. A.A. Adams of Kenora & Cecil Parsons, a most jovial pair. We had tea with them & what a merry meal it was. After tea, Gillis & I went fishing in a canoe on a very pretty lake at the south of the camp. Gillis indulged in a footbath while, I paddled. It is likely the lake will have to be dredged in consequence.

Parson's camp

Gillis and Jackman walked to Snell on Monday morning and had lunch at the new hotel, after which they trekked along Hawk Lake to a camp for supper, then to Margach. They spent the night in the station waiting room, a miserable experience! The brown walls did not lend a note of joy and the benches were hard. At least, however, they could smoke their pipes at the men's end. The women's end had a no smoking sign.

Stamps. June 11 Stamp and notations on left page.

By this time John had begun to know and to trust Charles. He told him about his difficulties with the loquacious and prevaricating George Cumming and George's eternal backup, Jack McDonald. He told Charles about how disgusted he was with their nightlife antics in Montreal, how he had broken up with them, and how he had changed his goal from San Francisco to Vancouver.

Charles listened supportively and smiled. "That was providential for me. There are so many ifs in this life. If Cumming hadn't been called away that January morning, with McDonald then becoming the third man, you'd probably be walking with Cumming toward San Francisco and trying hard to stomach his big talking. And I'd be walking all the way to Vancouver by myself without you to catch up to and walk with. That sounds selfish of me, but that's how I take it."

They tramped to Kenora, where the Lake of the Woods empties into the Winnipeg River, and stopped at the comfortable Commercial Hotel, owned by Mr. McVeigh. This was near the end of their walk over the Precambrian Shield, a land of water, forests, rugged wilderness and wildlife. Mr. McVeigh told the travellers that the Lake of the Woods had thousands of miles of shoreline and 14,000 islands. Once a fur trading post and a gold rush centre, Kenora owed its life to the Canadian Pacific Railway, which soon transported its timber, fur and fish to eastern markets. This was the land of the Chippewa First Nation, who continued to inhabit the territory and live on its game, fish, wild rice and berries.

Jackman on business, Kenora

While John was busy selling his souvenir cards, getting the
mayor's signature and writing letters, Charles spent an enjoyable time talking with Sergeant Egan of the Royal North West
Mounted Police, who had just returned from a perilous journey
to Ball Lake to bring back Aboriginal witnesses in a murder
trial scheduled to take place shortly in Kenora. Some time earlier, both Sgt. Egan and Sgt. McGuire (subsequently deceased)
had moved to arrest the suspect and lodge him in the Kenora
jail. That evening Charles devoted two and a half pages of his
small diary to that event and to "the finest body of men in the
world" – of which fifty percent were Englishmen, all of splendid

physique – and to their adventurous life. Besides clothing, a NWMP recruit earned sixty cents a day, and after five years, eighty-five cents. A corporal received a dollar a day, and a sergeant a dollar and a quarter. "A young man intending making his home in Canada could not do better than put in five years with the NWMP."

Jackman [centre] walking with Sergeant Egan of the NWMP.

Gillis wrote a letter dated June 13 to the Sporting editor of the *Post*,[2] wherein he revealed how he had been joined "before reaching Kenora by C.H. Jackman, a commercial traveller, who is well known in Cape Breton, and who was one of the international lacrosse players who formed the Toronto team that defeated the best players in England." The article stated: "Gillis writes in glowing terms of his mate, and says the Englishman's companionship has had a wonderful effect for the better on him, after travelling so far alone ... He says the bundle of *Posts* sent him were received at Kenora all right, and he appreciated them more than a letter from his best girl." One wonders what she thought when she read that.

Tunnel west of Kenora

Trudging for Winnipeg

Before leaving Kenora on Thursday, June 14, Jackman took snaps, which included two of the First Nations Aboriginals from Ball Lake. In the evening the travellers arrived at Deception (they did not know that this word was French for disappointment). Failing to find accommodation for the night, they tried again at a camp four miles on. While Gillis attempted to explain matters to a sleepy cook, Jackman was helping himself to a breakfast already prepared for the gang. He didn't say whether he had saved some for his hiking partner. Nothing to do but keep on trudging! Daybreak found the men at Ingolf refreshing themselves in a lake, then breakfasting in a section house. They lazed about, lunched, strode to Cross in Manitoba for supper and finished at 42-mile Post. The boarding car had no beds for them. They tramped round and round trying to keep warm until they had a chance to talk to, not with, a taciturn, unresponsive cook.

Finally, at long last they found a good breakfast that Saturday at Jolly Bars Camp; Culver for supper in a boarding car; and before midnight Whitemouth on a river of the same

Jackman, photographed by Gillis, June 14, 1906

name! Sunday, they rested, and had time to find out about Whitemouth, railway town and staging and supply centre. How proud the townsfolk were of their Dr. Charlotte Ross, the first woman Manitoban physician, who had long defied a ban on woman doctors in order to care for workers, Native peoples and new settlers. Gillis heard this as he spoke with residents on the street and sold a few souvenir cards.

— • —

Rain on Monday kept them indoors until early afternoon, when the trekkers decided to take the plunge. After a miserably wet trudge, they had supper at Julius and by midnight reached Beauséjour. The next day Gillis was surprised and pleased to meet a pugilist friend, Nath Campbell, from Glace Bay. John was all day in Beauséjour, while Charles witnessed the fights at no charge.

The noise made would lead one to imagine that several deaths would result at least but the only wound that I observed was a slight scratch on a Scotchman's face. Disgraceful farce from start to finish.

Another day behind them, the two made good time to Tyndall for lunch. In the rain they reached East Selkirk and ploughed through mud to West Selkirk, where they found comfortable quarters at the Canadian Pacific Hotel. Because Selkirk was "a dead sort of place," they were glad to leave after lunch. Friday, June 22, they came happily to Winnipeg and the

Strathcona Hotel. Jackman commented in his diary that since leaving Fort William they had lost much time and were several days behind. He was somewhat swollen from the bites of black flies, mosquitoes and sand flies.

Charles found that Winnipeg had grown considerably since he was there before. In fact it had doubled to 128,000 in five years and had grown from a mere 1,000 since its incorporation in 1875, when the main street was a muddy prairie trail. The great railway and grain centre of the west, with thousands of railway and elevator employees, was also a market for farm produce, fish, minerals and timber. Its wide streets were paved and its centre boasted an electric railway. The place was alive.

Holiday celebration on Main Street, Winnipeg

While in Winnipeg, Gillis had more souvenir cards printed. He spent all the time he could with his younger brother, Peter Dan, and other young men from Cape Breton who were doing well in Winnipeg. Ross Forbes, an executive of a wholesale stationery firm, was John Hugh's kind and generous host.

Jackman telephoned several companies in the hope of finding old friends but was disappointed to learn that they were all out of the city. Finding his footwear too worn to continue, he bought a pair of Slake boots.

— • —

Sunday, June 24, was a day of rest for both men. Gillis attended to mass and then, according to Jackman's diary, "miraculously disappeared." We know that John Hugh was being entertained by Ross Forbes, and that he was enjoying a reunion with his brother and friends from Cape Breton. The celebration plan seems to have happened so rapidly after mass that John did not have the opportunity to tell his partner. The following morning, Charles was trying to trace his baggage, sent from Kenora a week previous. That afternoon he was overjoyed to meet Allan Iler and Percy McBride, two old lacrosse friends, on Main Street. He had dinner with them. Jackman and Iler had played lacrosse for Stockport, England, and for Toronto.

On Tuesday Jackman's baggage turned up with much storage to pay. On Wednesday Charles was looking for John Hugh, who he found late Thursday. The two set out at 9 p.m. but were soon driven by a thunderstorm to seek shelter in the station house at Bergen. They caught a few hours sleep in the waiting room and left right after breakfast for Rosser, then Marquette,

McDonald Comes Home

The return of John McDonald on June 22 was announced by the *Sydney Daily Post*:[3]

PEDESTRIAN HOME

One of North Sydney's Famous Three Is Back to Home and Mother

Jack McDonald, the transcontinental pedestrian who, in company with Gillis and Cummings, left here on January 31 on a trip to San Francisco and return, on a wager of $600, arrived home Friday. According to McDonald, when he and Cummings parted from Gillis, they kept along the road until, hearing of the big disaster at San Francisco, they boarded the first freight headed toward the Pacific, finally landing in 'Frisco. They rode blind baggage as far back as Toronto, and beat the remainder of the way to Montreal, where McDonald and Cummings broke up the partnership, the latter remaining in the city, while McDonald kept along to Cape Breton. Jack looks pretty well after his trip, and apparently is happy to be home again.

This version of Jack's parting with George is different than the one he related in Quebec. Did the two really ride the rods to the devastated city of San Francisco and, if so, why? There is no way of telling. Jack was at Quebec the week of June 4 and was home by the 22nd, meaning he travelled eight hundred miles in eighteen days. In this latest story he used vague words such as "beat the remainder of the way" and "kept along." Was he walking or riding?

More interesting, there is no mention of his wife. What veiled meaning did the newspaper convey when it used the headline "Back to Home and Mother"?

Prairie Trails and Pioneers

After lunch at Poplar Point on Saturday, the last day of June, Gillis and Jackman took the muddy road to High Bluff. It was pouring rain. When, at nine o'clock, they reached Portage la Prairie on the CPR track, they looked in vain for accommodation. The hotel was crowded for the Dominion Day races. By good luck, they finally finagled their way into the Belle View. More thunderstorms on Sunday. The weather did not clear until four in the afternoon. The men had plenty of time to hear about early voyageurs on the Assiniboine River and the fur trading post of Fort la Reine, and, of course, the coming of the railway in 1880. John found time also to get the mayor's certificate.

Monday, July 2, Charles snapped MacGregor Station and the agent Mr. Giffin at lunchtime, after which he and John watched sports and had supper at Austin, and got into Sydney at nine. They arrived the next day at Carberry in the sand hills after walking over rolling topography. It was potato country!

Arrived Carberry for lunch & remained there until 11.30 p.m., when we started on an all night tramp. Mosquitoes were in evidence for several miles of the distance & the walk across the prairie was anything but pleasant, being an awfully wet & dark one. We made no stop all night & arrived in Brandon more dead than alive at 8.30 p.m. Dis. for day 47 miles.

Brandon, Manitoba, July 4, 1906

While Charles was spending time on Wednesday and Thursday with Dr. Robinson, an old friend, John was talking with residents on the street, purveying his souvenir cards, seeking the mayor's signature and strolling along the banks of the Assiniboine River. He learned curiously that this regional centre and CPR divisional point had descended from a

Hudson's Bay Company post called Brandon House (after the Duke of Brandon, an ancestor of Lord Selkirk). John also visited the federal agricultural research station. He wrote a letter to the *Post* about the very bad weather, Ross Forbes's wonderful hospitality and John's happy time with his brother and friends in Winnipeg. The paper turned it into an article with these headlines:[4]

GILLIS IS STILL PLODDING ALONG

EXPECTS TO REACH VANCOUVER BY AUGUST 15th

This Would Give Him Over Five Months
in Which to Get Back to North Sydney –
He Met Many Cape Bretonians in Winnipeg

—— • ——

Feeling very fit after their rest, the trekkers met a Yorkshireman who inhospitably forgot to invite them to dinner. By the time they arrived in Griswold, in the Sioux Valley, they were too late to get a meal and retired to bed hungry. Saturday was another hot day. They lunched and paused a few hours in the lively little town of Oak Lake. They plodded through the land of the Dakota Ojibwa in the heat until a tributary of the Assiniboine lured them to have a dip in its pristine waters.

On arriving at the latter place I was decidedly annoyed to discover the loss of my note book. Departed immediately after tea to hunt for it. Walked ten miles down the track & was fortunate enough to meet a section man who had picked it up.

CPR section men, Manitoba

They spent the day at Virden, where the sociable Charles met a number of men: Mr. MacMathers, a son of the chairman of Coates Mills in Paisley, Scotland – "remittance man of course" – a lawyer by the name of Wainwright who was three and a half inches taller than Charles, and also a son of Judge Savary of Annapolis Royal, Nova Scotia, who accompanied them for a mile on their way in the evening.

Cumming's return on Monday, July 9, was announced by the *Sydney Daily Post*:[5] another long-distance pedestrian "turned up yesterday from Montreal on the Black Diamond steamer *Cacouna*. It is no less than George Cumming, the famous musicologist, who has nothing left to say but that the distance did not lend enchantment to the view so he quit the tramping business and forfeited the right to try for the wager at Montreal."

GEORGE CUMMING CROSSED ATLANTIC

Cross Continent Traveller Says That He Got on the Wrong Boat

George Cumming, one of the cross-continent sprinters who did not cross the continent, and who arrived in the city the other day, tells some interesting tales of his experience during his absence, and tells them as only George can. One of his escapades was a clandestine trip across the Atlantic on the Allan liner *Sardinian*, which carried a cargo of cattle. George stowed away at Montreal, or, to use his own words, he got on the wrong boat.

"What could I do," said George, "when I made a mistake like that except to make the best of it? I was gazing out upon the sunrise in the early morning, when I heard someone say: 'All who want tobacco will come around at twelve o'clock.' Did I want tobacco? Well, say! When the hour arrived I was on the spot for my dope. That's where I made the mistake.

George goes on to say that he was spotted at once and charged with being a stowaway. This, of course, he indignantly denied, and asserted with all the eloquence at his command that he got his boats mixed. He was taken to the purser, and afterwards to the captain, who sentenced him to shovel coal into the boilers during the trip. "Well, captain," said George, "I won't be much good down there as I am paralysed on one side," and he gave a fine imitation of a man without the use of his right arm.

"Well, then," replied the captain, "you'll have to water the cattle."

George accepted his revised sentence with as much philosophy as he could under the circumstances, but found that the cattle drank too much water, and determined to cure them of that. He threw the bucket over the side and brought it up full of salt water. This, of course, the cattle refused to touch, and he gave the excuse to the head cattleman that his clothes smelled of carbolic acid, and that was probably the reason the cattle declined to drink. He was then sentenced to feed the animals with hay, which he did to the best of his ability until his arrival on the other side.

George saw King Edward and all the prominent statesmen of the empire during his vacation, and says he returned much improved in health.[6]

Heat and Poor Time

History was written for Charles Jackman at Hargreave when he ate his first piece of Yorkshire pudding since coming to Canada in 1902.

> *The heat has been simply terrible of late. Walking has been horribly hard work, too little shade & no breeze being the order of things. As a result of it all we are making distinctly poor time & I fear Vancouver will not see us until late in August. Arrived in Elkhorn for tea after a remarkable record of 8 miles.*

To make matters worse, Gillis and Jackman lost two days, flat broke, in Elkhorn. At last on Thursday, July 12, a glorious, cool day, Jackman received money from his company and they were able to get going again. They saluted the new province of Saskatchewan by dining in its border town of Fleming. They walked over rolling parkland and found beds at the Queen Hotel at Moosomin. Named for an Aboriginal chief, this community, which was founded when the construction of the Canadian Pacific Railway reached that point in 1882, boasted several general stores and hotels, livery stables and blacksmiths, doctor and lawyer, printer and butcher.

Jackman and Gillis at Grenfell, Saskatchewan

Charles and John followed a prairie trail to Wapella for lunch, where Charles had business until five o'clock. Then they trudged through a chill rain to Burrows for supper at the section house, and on to sleep at Whitewood after walking thirty-five miles. Whitewood, named for its groves of silver poplars, was a major CPR stop where people of British and many European nationalities came to settle. Leaving early Saturday, July 14, the men had a swim in a stream on their way to

Broadview for lunch, then a long pause out of the heat until nine o'clock, when they took a prairie trail and somehow in the dark got lost for a time. Finally they reached Grenfell and stopped at a comfortable hotel, The Granite.

Bunker Barlow

In Grenfell, Charles bumped into an old lacrosse chum, harking back to the English championship team on which they had played together! While John Hugh Gillis wandered around the lovely little town, talking to people and interesting them in his souvenir cards, Charles was enjoying himself chatting with "Bunker" Barlow about Manchester and the lacrosse players they had known.

Jackman with Bunker Barlow

Monday July 16. Desperately hot one. Slacked until night, taking several naps. In the afternoon Barlow conceived the notion that he'd like to finish the walk with us. No sooner was the notion conceived than he started an auction sale of all unnecessary baggage, out of which came much fun. He gave me a splendid little revolver, which I unfortunately lost an hour afterward & at 9 p.m. we left for Summerberry, three strong.

When the three left after breakfast, in the glorious morning, they saw the church and the two-storey school built of stone from a nearby quarry. Later they walked by a great marsh with its many birds. The travellers followed a good trail to Wolseley (named for the Lord Wolseley who helped end the Riel Rebellion at Batoche), where they admired houses, the courthouse and the combined town hall and opera house, all built of brick from the town's brickyard. This prairie town was unusual in that it was built around a lake the CPR had made by damming Wolf Creek. The men had a splendid lunch at a restaurant, in the shady garden of which they enjoyed a brief time off. Jackman took a picture of a suspension bridge over the dam.

Must have been intoxicated by the lovely western air, for I periodically chased gophers on the way to Sintaluta, much to the amusement of my co-pedestrians. Arriving at Sintaluta, we were ordered about the dining room by her majesty the waitress, who worked herself into a fever at the idea of mere men causing her to work later than 6.30. Girls are at such a premium out here that they practically run the show & if one should sit on them as I very often do most indiscreetly, a very poor meal results. Crowds assembled at the station to see us as we booked out for Indian Head.

It was "beastly hot" Wednesday, July 18, despite the trees that lined the streets. While Jackman did business with customers, Bunker relaxed and Gillis strolled around the Dominion Experimental Farm and the great tree nursery that provided shelterbelts for prairie farms. They left after lunch and walked along the prairie trail, before enjoying a refreshing swim in the river for an hour or so. Twelve miles took them over fescue grassland and woodland of alders to arrive for supper at Qu'Appelle on a river and in a valley of the same name.

The three hikers followed a roundabout trail in extremely hot weather. They had lunch with a Chester man who was joining up. A thunderstorm delayed McLean but they eventually reached Balgonie for tea, where Jackman bridled at the impertinence of a "squirt of a hotel man." They had a good old Yorkshire feast with people just arrived from Jackman's native shire. Bidding goodbye to their hosts at eight, the men followed the railway track to Regina, arriving at one in the morning. The day's walk was thirty-five miles.

Gillis Captures Regina

A beautiful day it was on Friday, July 20 in the "go-ahead town" of Regina. Another creation of the CPR in 1882, Regina was now lining its streets with trees to shade people from the glaring prairie sun. Charles remarked in his journal that Regina had doubled its population to 10,000 since he had been there two years before. Once the capital of the Northwest Territories, the city began to flourish as the capital of the new province of Saskatchewan in 1905. "The hotels of Regina have always been notoriously bad and I found the Lansdown even worse than it was two years ago." While Charles conducted his business over two days and renewed his acquaintance with Sergeant MacKinnon of the Royal North West Mounted Police, John Hugh got a certificate from the mayor and had more souvenir cards printed. His and Charles's interview with *The Daily Standard*[1] made centre front page with Gillis's photograph.

*"J.H. Gillis –
The giant Scotchman
who is walking from
ocean to ocean and
back on a wager, is in
Regina today."*

WALKING FROM OCEAN TO OCEAN

Scotchman Under a Wager to do Round Trip
on Shank's Pony Within Year

A Scotchman of surprising height, tanned to the red brown of the native, and with the free and easy bearing of the outdoor man, strode into the editorial sanctum this morning and announced himself as J.H. Gillis, from North Sydney, N.S., outward bound on Shank's Pony for Vancouver, and due to return on foot to his home on the Atlantic seaboard by Feb. 1 next or pay forfeit on a wager of $1,200. The progress of Mr. Gillis has been chronicled by the Canadian press as he has steadily pushed onward through thickly populated Nova Scotia and Quebec, bisecting Ontario, traversing the difficult North Shore country and debouching from Winnipeg onto the free and rolling prairie. He is six feet four and a half inches tall, weighed 195 pounds when he left home and now scales 12 pounds less, though he is looking fit and none the worse for the 2,700 odd miles he has already traversed. He carries with him notebooks containing official stamps of points he passes through, generally countersigned by the station agent for the Canadian Pacific in the silver thread he is following across the continent.

"And how do you stand now as to time?" he was asked.

"Well I am quite a bit behind owing to about six weeks trouble with sore feet which developed after I had been a month on the road. I left on Feb. 1 and have to get back within a year or lose the wager. I started penniless and the condition is that I may make my way from the proceeds of these post cards at ten cents a crack." Mr. Gillis here produced some of the cards in question, bearing ... the legend: "J.H. Gillis, transcontinental pedestrian from North Sydney, N.S., to Vancouver, B.C., and return within a year. Distance 7,680 miles."

"The rate we are making now," he went on, "is pretty good and if I can keep up an average of 27 or 28 miles a day I shall do all right."

Mr. Gillis has had a walking partner since Montreal (sic) in the person of a big Englishman, who curiously enough is exactly the same height, but C.H. Jackman is a vagabond for his health and intends returning by train from Vancouver. He looks in first class condition and tells *The Standard* that he is immensely benefited by the trip so far. He heard of Gillis after the latter had passed through Montreal, and, the spirit of the thing catching him, he started out at a good clip and caught up the Highlander and the two have travelled together ever since. Jackman weighs 196 pounds, though he scaled 225 pounds when he started.

At present they travel mostly by night owing to the heat, and they arrived in the city at an early hour this morning from Qu'Appelle, having covered 37 intervening miles as their day's work. Mr. Gillis expects to make a good deal better time on the return trip as he will know the route and will be able to pick up the friends he has made on the outward journey. The going will also be cooler and the steps fewer. A good deal of interest is being taken in the attempt by pedestrians throughout the Dominion

The Leader Post the same day had a small article[2] showing Gillis's picture and reporting that his father was a carpenter and builder and that J.H. had "done something at the same business." It went on to state that three years ago John had worked in the town of Revelstoke.

An hour before midnight, Bunker Barlow, John Gillis and Charles Jackman set out westward on the CPR track, which they abandoned at dawn for a prairie trail that led them through a slough up to their knees. The men squelched into Penno at four in the morning and bunked down in the Stefina Hotel after a toilsome trek. On Sunday, July 22, they ate breakfast and returned to their beds until lunch. They arrived in Moose Jaw as the clock at the CPR hotel struck twelve midnight. The next morning they viewed the town, sheltered in the valley where the Moose Jaw River and Thunder Creek meet. Moose Jaw was forging ahead and could boast two new hotels. The manager of the CPR Hotel asked them to lunch and the men spent the afternoon in the lovely hotel garden with the resident engineer. Leaving in the evening, they were soon driven back to town by a fierce thunderstorm back. They amused themselves with local residents, and Jackman tried to do a cartwheel he used to do so easily.

The next day, an extremely hot Tuesday, Jackman wheedled lunch of an egg and a prune apiece from the young woman in charge at the subdivision farm in Boharon. The walkers returned to the station, where they had left their luggage, and waited for the end of the storm. They decided to chance it at three o'clock, but thirty minutes later the renewed storm chased them back in a handcar.

Had tea & later had the misfortune to hear the Section Lounge Lady wrestle with her piano. She said she only played marches & waltzes. The marches were flung off like waltzes & the waltzes played like marches & the whole played like the devil. Barlow made me almost lose control of myself by telling her it was positively the finest & asked her if she could sing. I thereupon had an accident with the baby, who from then on needed all its mother's attention.

Finally, the men left Moose Jaw in the evening and soon reached Caron, a new and lovely town inhabited mostly by Americans. Charles Jackman, the businessman, was interested in a Mr. Steer, who had bought ten thousand acres from the CPR and then advertised a proposal whereby he would set up a farmer in operation with a quarter or half section of land and supply a comfortable house, barns and seed, and would break half the land. He would provide supplies at low prices, give two years to pay for them, and in return he would take half the crop for ten years.

Three Men Rough It and Frolic

The trekkers left Caron thirty minutes before noon on Wednesday and spent three hours "frolicking in a lovely lake, feeding up on biscuits and chocolate between dips." They "ran around like savages and had a thundering good time." They arrived in the new town of Mortlach, a lively spot, for dinner and left mid-evening. When they got to Parkbeg just before midnight and, finding there was "no accommodation for tramps," like true hoboes they found a haystack and had an enjoyable sleep. After a refreshing dip and a good breakfast, they followed the track to Secretan, had lunch and relaxed until four, before reaching Chaplin at seven:

More haystacks. Retired early & when we were snugly tucked up in the hay, we had a concert, Gillis being particularly good with sundry bagpipe selections . . . Had a rude awakening. Violent thunderstorm at 5 a.m. drove us out among the hens. We unkindly robbed them of a dozen eggs, which we proceeded to suck. Fortunate we were in having the eggs, for the breakfast we had later was disgusting. Walked to Ernfold in the morning, where we arrived broke & 'twas up to Jackman to make court to ye section house lady, which he did most successfully. Lost this precious book again in the afternoon, Gillis being at fault this time. We retraced our steps out on the prairie for four miles & the eagle-eyed Gillis spotted the dear little red thing almost buried in a gopher hole.

Apart from newspaper reports, that little diary is the only known written record of this long walk to have survived. The rest is oral history. When the men arrived at Morse, on Reed Lake, they were still without money. Luckily they met a friend of Charles's, Mrs. Daly, whose husband had been transferred from Dauphin to Morse. They had a "ripping tea at Daly's and huge sport with a rattling good gramophone." They left reluctantly at 9:30 and arrived at midnight in Herbert, where they found comfortable quarters in Herbert House.

— • —

The extremely hot Saturday, July 28, brought them feverish worries about how they were going to pay their bill but, fortunately were able to arrange later payment with the landlady.

Hoping to be asked for lunch, the trekkers walked south on a farm road to a family they had heard about. Humphrey and Alice Garfield welcomed them with Prairie hospitality. Years ago the Garfields had sold their farm in Prince Edward Island and come out west by train with their four little boys.

"When we arrived in Swift Current," Humphrey told his visitors, "I bought a pair of dappled grey geldings and a new wagon with a three deck box in which I loaded lumber, furniture, fuel, seed, food to last months, suitcases, blankets, dishes, and of course the family. Those wild horses ran twenty miles before they slowed down."

He proudly showed the three men the homestead, a mile long, and half a mile wide. A creek ending in a slough flowed through the middle length of the property. The men saw a herd of antelope and a flock of wild turkeys and, on a hill farther away, a red deer. When they returned to the ranch, young

"Slim" Garfield grasped his horse's mane with his left hand, put his right hand on the withers and leapt on the horse's back. "Slim" amazed the visitors when he jumped down and remounted on the fly on each side of the horse.

His father said, "Slim's a bit of a show-off, but he's good. He's been going bareback since he started riding to school at six. He can do just about everything with a lariat and he tames mustangs for the neighbours. You know, most of the horses we farmers use are wild off the range and they have to be broken. Their wildness causes accidents that end in injury or sometimes death."

After a hearty dinner, the three hikers thanked their hosts and walked to the track. When they got to Rush Lake they gave up on account of the horrific mosquitoes and slept on a boxcar floor. They had supper with an Englishman from Folkestone and stayed until ten o'clock, owing to a thunderstorm. Little more than a mile down the road, the renewed rain drove them to seek refuge in a hay barn, where they slept soundly.

Awoke fairly fresh considering the hardness of my couch, breakfasted at the section house & struck out at 8 a.m. After walking two miles we once again made Indians of ourselves & after mud baths and other kinds we went snake slaying, accounting for 36 between us. Was a glorious day & we were all as happy as sandbags. After four miles of grinding, a cool river of considerable depth tempted us & we played again, Barlow "missing" a tuck which we ought to have for lunch. Later in the afternoon we hiked us to a ranch & made love to a Scotch woman. We won a jug of milk and while the old girl was hunting for the cow juice, Barlow *(doubtless arguing that all is fair in love) pocketed half a dozen eggs. How beastly ungrateful! But he paid for it by swallowing a chicken lurking in the first egg.*

The next morning was cool when they left at five o'clock, walked across the railway bridge over the stream that gave its name to Swift Current, passed the dam, watersheds and freight sheds and sat down to a good breakfast. They lazed about in the great heat, which kept them off the road until seven in the evening.

The day's walk brought them to Seward, where, unable to find accommodation, they sloshed a mile through marsh to a haystack. Even covered by hay, they shivered as the cold of the dark night bit into their bones. Unable to find breakfast at Seward, they leaned into a high wind for five miles until they came to a construction camp. The old cook was cursing his broken-down stove, its maker and the whole set-up but he did relent enough to give the three hungry wayfarers some pie. At a camp farther on they "met an awfully decent chap from Cape Town." After lunch at Webb, they ran into a CPR engineer named Ogilvy, with whom they had a wonderful day playing baseball and engaging in other pursuits.

The night being beautifully moonlit, we struck out at 10 p.m. The mosquitoes however were very attentive. Coming to a dug-out a few miles west of Webb, we decided to stop there for the night. First making a "smudge" to clear the place of the pests, we gathered brush off the prairie & made a capital bed & slept peacefully.

The travellers hailed the month of August by walking to a camp for breakfast, before striding on to Gull Lake and its flocks of ducks, geese and quail – a good place to wash their clothes. The section man treated them royally at Rochdale. Finally, they came to a spot on the prairie where they could build a fire and camp for the night.

In the cold, grey morning of Thursday, August 2, the men set out at six o'clock and walked more than an hour in rain that soaked them to the skin. They found shelter and breakfast in a railway boarding car but went without lunch because they were broke. By dinnertime, they were so hungry that Jackman, taking advantage of a Dutch woman's difficulties with English, conned a flitch of bacon.

Having developed very sore feet, Bunker Barlow suffered tortures as they walked from Crane Lake to Maple Creek, where they arrived at midnight after a day trek of thirty-eight miles. There, during that long tomorrow, in spite of all the arguments that Jackman could muster, his friend decided to go back to Grenfell, Saskatchewan. Gillis was more understanding than Jackman, who wrote in his little journal: "Once again I have been disappointed in a brother Englishman. Barlow is a good fellow with a weakness." Gillis bit his tongue and stayed out of the tussle between the two retired athletes. Gillis knew about excruciatingly painful feet, but he had kept on because he had committed himself to the promoters of the long walk, to the community and, above all, to himself. Barlow, on the other hand, had decided to come along on a whim, and now called it quits when the pain became too much.

Having said goodbye to Bunker, Charles and John Hugh left after breakfast for Kincarth in fine, breezy weather. Then came a historic moment when they crossed the border into the year-old province of Alberta. Mr. Marshall, the station agent at Walsh, took them in and filled them with lots of good food. He told them how the town was named for Major James Walsh of the North West Mounted Police who had founded the fort. A friend of Sitting Bull, Walsh had provided sanctuary for the Sioux and paved the way for their return to the United States.

At midnight the visitors turned in for a few hours of rest. They had a tiresome walk on Sunday before they enjoyed an excellent breakfast at the Alberta Hotel, after which Jackman had a long-anticipated meeting with Sammy Gockier. His journal about the contretemps in the afternoon is cryptic but it seems that "in an absurd mixup fists were flourished & huge excitement prevailed" but no one was hurt. Sammy stayed with Charles for the night.

After a lazy morning and lunch, Charles, John and Sam walked to Jim Gaskell's Ranch at Many Island Lake but they went six miles extra because Sam, *naturally*, took the wrong trail. They met young Mrs. Gaskell and their boy Sam. They had a great deal of fun before the visitors bunked down on the floor.

Charles spent much of Tuesday chatting with Sam about old times. He noted that Sam was much fatter than he had been in Toronto three years ago. John Hugh provided much fun by discovering that his host, Jim Gaskell, "was very foolishly robbing himself of 80 acres." Jim had shown him the deed. After quietly studying the boundaries, John Hugh made quite an act of showing Jim how he was short-changing himself.

Having breakfasted at 3:30 in the morning, Jim Gaskell set off for the station with Sam, who was going to Chicago, and with Gillis and Jackman, who were heading for Irvine. At Irvine, Charles and John breakfasted a second time and fully intended to leave after lunch, but cowpunchers and horse breakers so captured their attention that they didn't get away until after supper. The darkness and the poor railway track caused them to give up at the Paisley Pit boarding car. Charles declared the man in charge was the most bitter, lackadaisical man he had ever met.

When on Thursday, August 9, they arrived at lunchtime in Medicine Hat, they were too late to say goodbye to Sammy, who had already left for Chicago. Neither Jackman nor any of the friends of Sam ever heard from him again. Some time later

Bridge at Medicine Hat, Alberta

Jackman instituted a police search in Chicago but Sam was gone without a trace!

Heat and Bad Water

Charles took the Slake boots he had bought in Winnipeg to the shoemaker to be resoled after seven hundred miles of hard walking. Charles was minding the heat, and felt rather sick from all the alkali water he had drunk. As usual John Hugh got the mayor's certificate, had more souvenir cards printed and gently hawked some in conversation with passers-by. The inhabitants were proud of their growing tree-shaded town, which had started in 1883 as a collection of tents around the new CPR station in a valley of the South Saskatchewan River. The men made only twelve miles that day!

The tremendous heat kept them from starting out until mid-afternoon. As they crossed the bridge over the big river, Jackman took a photo. At a magnificent ranch owned by Mr. Burke, they had supper and stayed the night. By Saturday the unforgiving heat led to unquenchable thirst and the intake of so much alkaline water, that Charles felt himself getting worse. After lunch at Bowell the two spent time listening to a gramophone and talking with CPR agent Casey, who had played lacrosse with the Toronto team the year before. It was 103 degrees Fahrenheit in the shade, or just about 40 degrees Celsius, when they departed and, on arrival at eight in Suffield, Jackman was "fagged out and distinctly sick." Sunday, Monday, and Tuesday were the hottest days ever with a wind that burned Gillis's face when he stepped out while Jackman recovered.

The men tried to make up lost time on Wednesday, August 16, as Charles was feeling a little better. They strolled to Langevin for lunch in the fiercely hot weather, stopped for water on the way to Tilley, where they had supper and a smoke with their pipes, and completed their "extremely strenuous" long walk at Brooks. The tired transcontinental pedestrians took it easy Thursday morning, before walking to Cassils, where they spent the night in the CPR camp.

During a relaxed morning on Friday, they enjoyed talking with Mr. Fong, the cook, who had been seventy-eight years on this continent and disliked the Canadian prairie. Fong's comment, as rendered in Jackman's diary, was, "No tlee, no lock, lotten countly!"

Having taken a photo of the men at the camp, Jackman and Gillis had supper in Latham. At Bassano, not able to get accommodation, they found a haystack that furnished little sleep during the very cold night.

The cool and lovely Saturday morning they walked to Crowfoot for lunch. "Got my first glimpse of the Bow River & what a treat it was to look at that lovely valley after the beastly

Bow Valley near Calgary

monotony of the prairie." Following the river and taking snap-shots, the men came at last to Gleichen and the first hotel they had seen since Medicine Hat, 130 miles back. This time they would have to pause because John Gillis was now decidedly unwell.

— • —

On Sunday, August 19, 1906, Charles Henry Jackman spent an unusually quiet birthday, his twenty-eighth, in a most interesting little town. "The Blackfeet Indians have a reserve just across the track & a truly picturesque crowd they are." This was the Reserve of the Siksika Nation of the Blackfoot Confederacy, who not long since had hunted the thundering bison. Gleichen was another little town, created in 1883, around a Canadian Pacific station, and was named for a finan-cial supporter of the railway company, Count Albert Gleichen, a visitor to the area. This divisional point was an important stop for all trains serving ranchers and homesteaders. "Crowds of cowpunchers are here spending Sunday."

Gillis was much better on Monday but rain kept them from starting until well after lunch. The trekkers walked along briskly and even more so as a violent rainstorm drenched them on the track to Strangmuir, where they finished a soggy hike. Tuesday, very stormy with a strong western wind and a heavy rain, they spent "watching cowboys loading cattle for P. Barbour & Co." Fine, cool weather prevailed when they left after breakfast the next day, and at last enjoyed dinner at a good hotel in Shepard.

We got our first view of the Rockies . . . at Langdon. They seemed very near though they were nearly 100 miles away & what a treat it was, for it told us of a break in the terrible monotony that comes of a 1000 mile grind over the prairie, of good drinking water & here and there a bit of trout fishing.

The men arrived at Calgary in the dark after ten o'clock Wednesday, August 22, and stopped at the Royal Hotel. They had tramped thirty-six miles that day and had a great feeling of accomplishment as they finished one more stage in their journey and prepared for the foothills and the mountains.

Foothills and Mountains

Yes, John Hugh Gillis and Charles Henry Jackman, marathon walkers, were in Calgary and happy to be there. Jackman wrote in his diary, "Calgary has grown tremendously since I was last here & also improved considerably, quite the nicest city in the west & the fact that it is so close to the Rockies gives it additional charm." They spent the whole of Thursday, in Calgary and had a good time. They were fascinated by its history, going back to the Blackfoot, Sarcey and Stoney and the bison kills, going back to the American whisky traders who set up forts and traded abominable alcoholic mixtures for buffalo robes and who expedited the formation of the Northwest Mounted Police to establish law and order.

One of the police forts was Calgary, probably a Gaelic word, Gillis was glad to hear, meaning "Bay Farm." The CPR was the moving force behind the town when it laid out the site in 1883. Jackman and Gillis were soon aware of how important the open-range cattle business was to Calgary. Coming off the prairie, they lingered along the Bow River. Gillis went to the mayor's office for a signature, got more souvenir cards printed, and talked with Calgarians about his long walk.

To the Great Divide

Finding it hard to leave Calgary, the men eventually said good-bye on Friday at 2:30. They had not gone far before rains cascaded down again. They had a very wet tramp to Keith. After a good steak in a boarding car, they plunged back into the rain, which kept coming down until they were a few miles from Cochrane, whereupon a strong cold wind chilled them to the marrow.

Saturday brought a glorious morning. Following the beautiful Bow Valley, they arrived in Morley at mid-afternoon, a time when lunch was not served. When Charles convinced the already sympathetic wife of the storekeeper that they were dying of hunger, she prepared a remarkably good meal. The two hikers spent an hour talking "with Indians in all sorts of wonderful costumes." Jackman took a photo of a stalwart brave. "We were now getting close to the Rockies & neither of us spoke very much. After the cruel walks on the prairie, the beauty of it all was very soothing & restful." They ate a picnic supper of crackers and cheese by the rushing Kananaskis River and soon reached Exshaw.

— • —

Anthracite, Alberta

On Sunday, August 26 the walkers set out after breakfast in fine, cool weather. "The scenery as one gets a few miles west is simply superb. In fact Gillis almost fell off a bridge, so busy was he ogling the Three Sisters." When they came to Anthracite at six, the men were so ravenous that they persuaded "the inhabitant" to cook them a meal. At Banff they settled in the King Edward Hotel. Norman Luxton, the proprietor, had met Jackman from a previous business visit. The next day they had a wonderful time in Banff, mostly taking pictures. The morning after, when the rain let up, the men ate lunch with the section foreman at Sawback and tried their luck fishing.

Banff National Park, Alberta

The afternoon was beautiful as we ambled westward & the scenery superb. To the south was the noble peak Pilot Mountain so called I believe because of its excellence as a landmark. Doubtless many a white man, and many a red, has muttered his thanks as he caught sight of that unmistakable peak. To the north we had Castle Mountain, perhaps the most beautiful mountain in the Rockies. It is 9500 feet above sea level & extends eight miles. It towers a sheer precipice 5000 feet above the track. We took tea at Castle Mountain & had the company of an awfully funny old Irishman.

It was moonlight when we started out, with our pipes going and as happy as sandbags. We followed the lovely Bow & enjoyed the finest scenery the eye could scan. Lovely enough in the sunlight, it is doubly so in the silvery rays of the moon. At 10 p.m. we sat down on the banks of the Bow to smoke and marvel at the grandeur of it all. It charmed us so much that we decided to build a fire & camp there for the night. With the moon peeping over the mountains & here & there a cloud trying to frown at the mountains, with the moonlit Bow at our feet, we reclined on our couch of boughs & spiny brush, warmed by a roaring fire, we blew baccy & thought how good it was to be alive.

An early jaunt brought them to Laggan for breakfast on that perfect day, Wednesday, August 29. They paddled in the river an hour or two and then, six miles farther, ate their lunch at the Great Divide, the summit of the Canadian Pacific Railway. There a rustic arch spanned a stream to mark the place where the waters divide. The Bow River departed for Hudson Bay while the Kicking Horse River left for the Pacific. Like an exuberant schoolboy with a sense of history, Jackman carved his initials on the arch. They decided that the scenery on the way to Field was perhaps the finest in the Rockies, while noting many safety switches as the track running through Kicking Horse Pass dropped 1,200 feet in eight miles. Jackman snapped several photographs. Fearing that they would be late for dinner, the two men marched the last mile in ten minutes. They had crossed their last border, into British Columbia.

Above: Kicking Horse Pass, Alberta
Below: A natural bridge near Field, Alberta

Rough Tracks and Long Bridges

Making a late start the next day, the trekkers had the hotel make them a lunch, which they ate beside a brook at Otterstad. They had a horrid walk over rough track wherein the ballast used was coarse gravel spread more often on the ties than between them. Reaching Palliser in the rain they found food and shelter, after much searching, in a hunter shanty. The last day of August was fine and cool as they followed the CPR through Kicking Horse Canyon, stopping now and then to take pictures. The men reached Golden in the broad valley of the Columbia, where they had a good lunch at the Queens Hotel. Mid-afternoon the rain spilled down on them as they made for Moberly. They found shelter with a farmer but, having no blankets to keep them warm, kept a fire going all night. Charles fuelled himself with tapioca pudding. How important it was to find food regularly to fuel the energy required for long walks every day!

On Saturday, September 1, Charles and John left the farm in doubtful weather, which cleared as they arrived at Donald. At Bearmouth, people treated them to a dinner. Soon they came to the end of the beautiful Columbia Valley and the ascent of the Selkirks, a place of grand scenery. "The Beaver dashes madly down steps hewn irregularly in the rock. The ravine closes in narrowly & at one point from either bank sheer solid rocks jut out stretching across the stream in great resemblance to the gates of a lock." Charles took several pictures of the bridge crossing the Columbia River and one of the Beaver Ravine.

Above: Crossing the Columbia River

Below: Beaver Canyon, B.C.

Following supper at Cedar, the travellers had a perilous walk to Bear Creek, as the railway track crossed many deep ravines. In the dim light they found it not only difficult to negotiate bridges but also impossible to hear an approaching train above the roar of the water. At Stoney Creek, the worst bridge of all was five-hundred feet long across a gully three-hundred feet deep. Despite, these obstacles the walkers negotiated over thirty-five miles that day. Such perils were to be taken with great care, for the pedestrian's lives were at stake. Once they came suddenly upon a huge bear, the first they had seen in the Rockies, but stayed well out of his path. There was no place to sleep at Bear Creek. So "they smoked the night away on the waiting room floor," talking desultorily about sports and books and life experiences, until about two in the morning when a train wreck added unusual excitement.

Next day, the two walked through numerous snow sheds on their way to Rogers Pass. Without food for fourteen hours, they were so ravenous that they found great joy and relief in meeting that "truly good sort," W.D. Morris, who kindly invited them to lunch. He told them how Rogers Pass got its name when, a quarter of a century ago, a Major Rogers found the long-sought route through the Selkirk Mountains.

— • —

With warm hearts and pleased stomachs, the two pedestrians said goodbye to their friends in Rogers Pass and headed for Illecillewaet. They had a miserable hike through Glacier over a wretched track roadbed to Ross Peak, where their spirits were lifted by an enjoyable supper with stranded walkers, Mrs. Kennedy of Illecillewaet and Mrs. Pratt of Revelstoke. Then the two adventurers waited for moonlight before they started on what turned out to be a most eventful walk – for they had to go though a tunnel three-quarters of a mile long. Since the train wreck at Cedar had been cleared earlier that afternoon, stalled trains were now making up lost time. Charles and John took chances but with lots of luck and long matches called lucifers they managed with only one accident, when John tripped into a culvert and barked his shin.

Snow sheds near Rogers Pass, B.C.

When the men arrived in Illecillewaet, everybody was abed. Mr. Mooney, the station agent, roused Mr. Wong, who found them a place for the night. "Wong seemed greatly exercised over our gigantic stature and when I asked him how he'd like to be as close to the stars as we were, he grinned and said, 'Alla same, long men, both long, thin like a bloom.'" The two tired men felt good to be once again between sheets. After walking so many miles a day their bodies cried out for sleep.

Monday the third was a glorious day, and after breakfast, the walkers enjoyed the scenery and took pictures on their way to Albert Canyon. They had lunch in the comfortable shack of a pleasant Scot named Fred Forrest, a most interesting fellow who had spent several years in the Congo. They were so enthralled by his tales that, as they were leaving with great reluctance, they discovered four hours had gone by.

They had supper with Mr. Waller, the watchman, "an awfully nice little Englishman." When he told them that he had been in San Francisco at the time of the earthquake and fire, they listened silently as he described what he had seen and felt. They had read about the disaster but here it was in vivid, searing detail.

In glorious moonlight, the two men made a most memorable walk through the Illecillewaet valley and canyon where there was a log crib dam. Charles and John arrived at Revelstoke, on the banks of the Columbia River, at midnight. The hotels were packed for the races and no beds were available. Drained from fatigue, they were relieved to get a room, at last, at five in the morning.

Sojourn in Revelstoke

John and Charles had planned to get repairs done in Revelstoke but when they awoke on Tuesday, September 4, they found that day to be a general holiday and all the shops were closed. Nothing to do but join the crowd, despite the dull weather! They found that Revelstoke had grown a good deal since they were there before. A fine station replaced "the old shack" that the CPR had built at the founding of the town in

1882. Now in 1906, Revelstoke was the "Capital of Canada's Alps" and a "Mountain Paradise." The traveller could take trains from that divisional centre north, south, east and west.

Rain spilled down the following day. The two hikers had nothing better to do than to go to repair shops, do some washing, get a certificate from the mayor, and stay in the hotel out of the rain. Fortunately they met Mrs. Atkins and Mrs. Pratt again and were happy indeed to be invited to the Pratt home for dinner, where they had a fine time talking with Mr. and Mrs. Atkins, Mrs. Pratt and Mr. Pratt, a native of London, Ontario, and manager of the Molson Bank in Revelstoke.

The next two days the rain fell without cease. As Charles and John talked with residents in the hotel lounge, they heard much about Revelstoke, how it was named for a lord who, as the head of an English bank, made a loan to the CPR when the railway was running out of money. There at "Big Eddy," people canoeing down the treacherous Columbia River stopped for a rest and there, too, came those who sought adventure in the Big Bend Gold Rush of the mid 1860s. Aboriginal peoples visited the town in the autumn to get salmon and huckleberries and always left before the deep snows and avalanches.

By 1906, Revelstoke had had electricity (installed eight years earlier), an Imperial Bank, and thirteen sawmills supplying the railroad. John Gillis had worked at one sawmill three years before. Canadian Pacific paddle wheelers transported freight south on the Columbia River, while private boats made trips north and south with mail, livestock, fresh produce, and people. Boats travelling north dropped picnickers off at the hot springs, but could steam only as far as LaPorte, just south of Death Rapids.

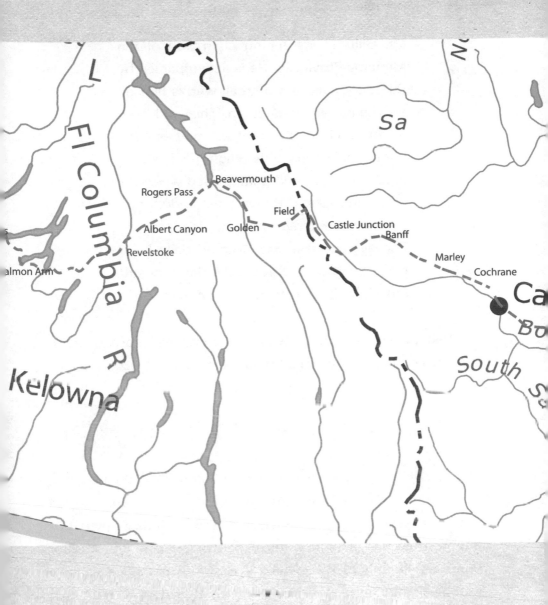

The *Revelstoke Mail-Herald* of Saturday, September 8, carried a news item[1] entitled "Transcontinental Tramps." The chief bits of new information were:

Just below this article was one about widespread heavy rains accompanied by violent windstorms.

The Last Spike and a Hermit

The inactivity of four days of delay was more than the two men could stand. Finally, they plunged into the rain, and passed wetlands where many birds nested and rested. Soaked but happy, they had a midday meal at the camp of the Mindry Lumber Company in Three Valley. The wet walk to Craigellachie was hard going over execrable, recently raised track. The men paused to look at the monument marking the driving of the last spike of the Canadian Pacific Railway. They felt a shiver as they gazed at that important accomplishment in the young life of the new nation.

After supper in the village, they set out, but the track and the light were so bad that after thirty-three miles they "chucked it for the night at Malakwa & put up with an old trapper by name Lidstone, a fine old recluse from P.E.I." Lidstone's father was a sailor from Dartmouth, Devon, who had settled at West Devon in the western part of the Island. Restless like his father, Lidstone had come to the mountains to enjoy the quiet life of trapping. He lived simply in his ramshackle cabin and liked to be alone but didn't mind the very occasional visitor with whom he could yarn a while. He told them about his life there and listened to the saga of their long walk. Why a man would walk so many miles day after day just for the fun of it made him scratch his grey head.

Lidstone's shack, Malakwa, B.C.

Got a snap of Lidstone, self & shack before leaving at 8 a.m. The track was still in awful condition & we had a strenuous twelve miles, arriving at Sicamous at 11.30. Got a lunch put up at the CPR hotel & ate it by Shuswap Lake an hour later. Shuswap is I think the finest lake in BC. It has arms like an octopus, some of which extend in various directions for miles. One follows Shuswap Lake for fifty miles, the scenery all along being very beautiful.

Had tea five miles east of Salmon Arm and such a tea. If I live to be a hundred I shall never forget it. I fear I made rather a hog of myself but truly I don't feel guilty, for Gillis was even worse. In fact when I think of the lovely rich gravy — of which there was an abundance — of the old fashioned rice pudding & the lovely apple sauce & the cream, it makes me rather regret I had no room for more. Norwegian people, and a sixteen years residence in BC did not make the good wife forget how she did things in the old country.

Arriving in Salmon Arm, we got mixed in the dark & running against a fence I fear I used some very strong English. A voice, obviously that of a fellow country-man, suggested that were I to climb the fence I should find a road that would take me to a hotel & at the same time proffered his senses as a guide. I fear I thanked the unknown somewhat ungraciously but one might be excused for mistaking a Church of England parson for a nobleman in Canada. In the dark a minute *later, had his reverence been the nobleman I took him to be, I think there would have been more strong English used, for he went up to his knees in mud. He proved to be a ripping little chap, Venables, & very good looking. He had read about our tramp and was delighted to meet us. We had a very enjoyable two hours before he left for the Okanagan Valley, where he resides.*

That Monday morning Charles and John followed the very bad track to Hatch Hill. On the way Gillis ran after a young eagle that had not learned to fly and, as it was fluttering over rocky terrain, he captured it. Wrapping it in a shirt with its head sticking out and squawking, he took it to the station, arranged for it to be fed and watered in an express car, and sent it to his brother-in-law Donald Parker. Whatever he thought of this, Jackman remained silent. They went on for supper at a boarding car and stopped at Shuswap, where they had trouble finding a place to sleep. At last they were able to rouse a farmer who had gone to bed early.

A memorable, rather warm day for the two long-distance walkers was Tuesday, September 11. Following the South Thompson River through the deep valleys of the ranching country, they had lunch near Monte Creek with Hon. H. Bosford at his ranch, where they met Constable W.L. Fernie of the Royal North West Mounted Police.

Fernie led the posse that captured Bill Miner, the incurable bandit of stagecoaches and trains. Miner left school at sixteen and as a pony express rider during the American Civil War he made good money, which he spent on booze and women. To support that easy life he robbed Wells Fargo Express of $75,000. The repeated holding up of stagecoaches got him many years in prison. When he came out at age fifty-five in 1903, stagecoaches were no more, but the film *The Great Train Robbery* gave him an idea. After a botched attempt on an Oregon train, he slipped over the Canadian border. At Mission on the rainy night of September 10, 1904, his partner Jake Terry, a former railway man, climbed a pole and telegraphed, "Combination lost. Leave safe open on train." They got from the uninsured, Canadian Pacific Railway much cash and gold dust and £50,000 in bearer bonds, which Miner buried.

Miner's admirers began to call the gentleman bandit, who apologized to his victims for the inconvenience, "Grey Fox." In Princeton, the polite, charming, storytelling Miner, aka "George Edwards" danced with women and gave children oranges. Despite posters, wire messages and a large reward, he remained free. If he had left it at that, people round might have continued to cultivate a deaf ear and a blind eye. Near midnight, however, on May 8, 1906, Bill Miner, Louis Colquhoun, a quiet teacher from Collingwood, Ontario, and "Shorty" Dunn, a hardware clerk, tried to rob the CPR *Imperial Limited* at its stop at Monte Creek. They raided the baggage car instead of the express car and got only $15. On July 1 Bill Miner was sentenced to New Westminster penitentiary for life.[2]

Bill Miner, the "Grey Fox"

After listening to this fascinating story, Charles and John said goodbye to the senator and Constable Fernie at 1:30. They had a picnic supper of crackers and marmalade at Mile Post 118 and reached Kamloops rather fatigued from a long, difficult tramp. In four days they had covered 130 miles "over a disgusting track."

Lively Kamloops

How glad they were on Wednesday, September 12, to have a day of rest and relaxed activity in the "busy little town of 2000 and a great ranching centre." A lively place at the confluence of the North and South Thompson Rivers, Kamloops was replete with hotels, stores, churches, schools, a hospital, a volunteer fire department, and telephone, water and electricity systems. Because the town was incorporated, Gillis went to see the mayor while Jackman conducted his business. Gillis had more souvenir cards printed, spoke with residents about his long hike and, of course, exchanged souvenirs for cash. He met some ranchers whose horses and cattle thrived on the climate and the bunch grass of the range. He also talked with lumbermen from the mills, but most often, he gossiped with workers of the Canadian Pacific Railway and those off the paddlewheel boats. Also in town were Shuswap Indians who had long hunted,

Kamloops, B.C.

fished and picked berries in the region and wintered in pit-house villages.

Jackman wrote a long letter to the Sporting editor of *The Toronto Star*, reviewing his experience since he had last written from Port Arthur at the end of May:

I was warned at Medicine Hat to keep a sharp lookout for rattlesnakes, which are supposed to be very plentiful between there and Calgary, but, although every man I met had slain countless thousands that very week, I failed to see even a dead one or to hear anything louder than the rattle of a grasshopper on the whole trip. I presume I travelled in peculiar luck.

To go through the Rockies by train is a vast treat, and one is greatly impressed by the grandeur of the scenery. I have made several such trips and thought I had seen all there was to be seen, but one doesn't realize the glory of it all until one walks through. To look at the mountains on either side of me for some time and to then continue walking makes me feel very much akin to a caterpillar crawling over a tent.

I had heard much — prior to reaching the mountains — of the ferocity of the bear and the mountain lion, or cougar. This, I find, is absolute "tommy-rot." Bears will not molest you unless wounded or unless you chance to stumble across one with cubs. An old trapper that I have met told me that the cougar is really the most cowardly of animals.

I have seen several bears, but as I am only armed with a revolver of such light calibre that a bullet there from would scarce part the hair of a jack-rabbit, I have not chanced a shot. Then, again, they seemed bent on avoiding me, and I rather liked their independent spirit.

I expect to be in Toronto again by the end of September.

Interestingly, Charles Jackman did not mention John Gillis, his walking companion and close friend, in his letters to *The Toronto Star*. Did he believe that the arrangement he had made with that newspaper had to do only with his progress and experiences across the country? Did he think that mentioning Gillis would require explanation that would take up too much space? Was he, a retired athlete, envious of the younger man? Or was it that his diary and his newspaper communications were his show alone? Gillis was able to report for himself at Regina and back home in Cape Breton. Though good friends, it seems one friend did not encroach on the other's space.

— • —

Following the rugged shores of Kamloops Lake westward on Thursday morning, they delighted in a perfect track. They walked through semi-arid grassland and over hills in "disturbingly hot" weather to finish at a comfortable hotel in Savona. On Friday, they arrived at Ashcroft located in a valley beside the great Thompson River. That town of five hundred was doing much business with the Cariboo district, for many heavily laden teams were moving along the trail. The two walkers left Ashcroft mid-afternoon Saturday, September 15, and soon found themselves forging southward on a dreary, lonesome stretch of CPR track in Thompson Canyon. They spent the night in Spatsum at the ranch of the "two veterans," Campbell and Wood, who treated them exceedingly well.

A three hours' march took them to Spences Bridge at the meeting of the Fraser and Nicola Rivers. At a so-so lunch and during a restful pause, they learned that some forty years ago Thomas Spence, famous road builder, completed the Cariboo Road with a wooden toll bridge across the surging Thompson River.

During the blazing hot afternoon, the two men slowly trudged to Thompson Siding, where they snacked on crackers and jam by a lovely spring. They delayed their departure until nightfall and reached Lytton at eleven. The darkness and the unusual layout of the streets delayed their finding the hotel but they were immediately welcomed by the proprietors, who, with others, wanted to hear about the experiences of the two famous walkers.

John and Charles were no longer pushing themselves to make time but were taking this tramp across the country as a lark, finding pleasure in people, in the overwhelming scenery and even in their vicissitudes. Gillis had some time ago realized that he had consumed more than half of the 366 days of the wager on the first half of the there-and-back journey. Indeed the arrival in Lytton marked 229 days of his outward hike.

Great heat, heavy rain, some sickness, business calls and many interesting acquaintances had slowed their progress. The two men had slipped into an easy and deep friendship, into an exchange of confidences: one, an athlete in retirement who would prove his strength and endurance in one last great adventure, and the other, much younger and with years before him in track and field, matching the determination and enjoying the humour of his companion.

Hell's Gate

They spent three enjoyable days in Lytton, talking with "a truly excellent bunch" of men and their wives. Both Charles and John were surprised to hear that the town was named for Sir Edward Bulwer-Lytton, whose novels, *The Last Days of Pompeii* and *The Last of the Barons*, they had read. Bulwer-Lytton was a rival of Dickens. However, it was not for the author who had written, "The pen is mightier than the sword," that the town had been named, but for the same man in his role as Secretary of State for the Colonies.

Gillis, of course, saw the mayor for his signature and renewed and merchandised his supply of souvenir cards. While he was busy with these affairs, Jackman spent the hot and windy Tuesday taking pictures along the Fraser River. On the glorious Wednesday they wandered up the Thompson River to do some fishing.

The two travellers said goodbye to their friends, who let them go with all sorts of good wishes. A few miles out of Lytton, they came to a remarkable cantilever bridge 530 feet long with a central span of 315 feet. Constructing it was very difficult because the site could be approached from only one end. Jackman wrote in his journal, "One half of the materials were sent across the river on a steel cable one and a quarter inches in diameter. Several pieces of the structure weighed five tons."

Walking almost due south on the track, they had lunch at Keefers and then a pleasant stroll to North Bend.

An early start on Friday, September 21, brought them soon to Hell's Gate, the granite throat that squeezes tightly the flow-through of the Fraser River. Charles got a good photograph of Hell's Gate, the very beginning of Fraser Canyon, down which the route is a veritable cliffhanger. Jackman wrote: "The track runs through unnerving tunnels & across several lofty bridges. The longest of the tunnels is 1000 feet and of the bridges 800 feet. From White Creek Bridge owing to a peculiar bend in the line one can see no less than six tunnels." Through those tunnels and over those high bridges they sped with their ears cocked for the deadly sounds of an approaching train.

Fraser River, B.C.

Hell's Gate, Fraser Canyon, B.C.

As they finished their lunch at Spuzzum, the little daughters of the section mistress gave them bouquets of flowers. The two men washed pairs of socks in a stream and continued their walk down the canyon, where the river cuts "through a lofty range of mountains thousands of feet below their summits." Charles Jackman wrote in his diary Friday, September 21:

Between the sharp projections which occur frequently there are deep lateral gorges, canyons & plunging cataracts. One of the most difficult problems has been to bridge these mountain torrents that in spring rush down the steep gorges of the mountain side like an avalanche; often on the lower side they drop hundreds of feet below the track.

In this section of 54 miles a construction army of 7000 men worked. During the building of this road, men were suspended by ropes hundreds of feet below the tops of the cliffs to blast a foothold! Supplies were packed in on the backs of mules & horses and building materials often had to be landed on the opposite bank of the stream & taken across at great expense.

Stamps, Sept. 20, 21, etc.

Fraser Canyon

And so down the formidable but glorious Fraser Canyon, the two travellers finally came to Yale, a site of ancient Aboriginal encampments, a former fur trading fort and a lively centre during the Fraser River Gold Rush. Rising early the next day, Charles and John stopped to fish for salmon. They lunched at Hope, where the Fraser sweeps widely toward the west and where the snow-capped Cascade Mountains form a breathtaking backdrop. Wrote Jackman, "Hope is really a beautiful spot & many people took up land under the impression that Hope would become a great tourist resort. It isn't but they still live in Hope." They picnicked in the rain under a bridge and got to Aggazie at nearly nine. They crossed a very long bridge in the pitch dark. When they were halfway across they met a train. "Fortunately we were near a step off and got nothing worse than a very good shaking."

Torrents of rain kept them in until afternoon on Sunday. They had a pleasant time with "two very good sorts," Captain Hamilton and Mr. Fife of *New York Life*. At two o'clock Gillis and Jackman decided to plunge into the heavy rain and, after a wet and strenuous trudge through forests, over hills, and by lakes and streams, arrived at Mission in the heart of the Fraser Valley.

Mission Junction railway station, B.C.

Journey's End

On the historic Monday, September 24, 1906, they left Mission in fine weather and high spirits. "We were for all the world like a couple of school boys & had great fun over really very little." They had lunch by a spring and got to Western Junction for supper. After a day's tramp of forty-two miles, they marched triumphantly into Vancouver Station at midnight. The telegraph must have been busy, for a crowd gave them a rousing reception and gazed upon them in wonder. Later, many gathered around a shoe store window, where Charles Jackman's walking boots were exhibited.

Charles Jackman immediately told his diary how he felt:

I can hardly realize that it's all over. It seemed as though there could be no end, first of that stretch of 1200 miles alone & then the horrible grind across the parched alkali plain with my good friend Gillis & lastly the trip through the Rockies with its glorious scenery, its lofty bridges & numerous tunnels. Here at last & how good it is to sniff the brine again, to live in decent clothes & to eat decent grub. No more stumbling over the beastly ties in the inky darkness, no more dashing across bridges to avoid trains, no more groping my way through black tunnels, no more wondering whether that bear I hear crashing through the bushes in the dark will come my way. All over, I have crossed a large part of the Dominion on foot and am well, for which I thank God frequently. Amen.

Transcontinental Pedestrians 229

half way over. fortuna[tely]
we were near a slag off
+ got nothing worse tha[n]
a jolly good shaking
Dist for Day 37 miles

Sept 23/06

It was raining in
buckets full when we
awoke + kept it up until
late in the afternoon
we had very good fare
in Capt. Hamilton +
Mr Fife (New York Life)
with whom we spent a
very pleasant morning.
It was raining quite
heavily when we left
for Mission Junction .
2 P.M.
After a most
strenuous walk over Gave
a last we arrived a[t]
Mission Junction 10 PM
Dist 39 miles

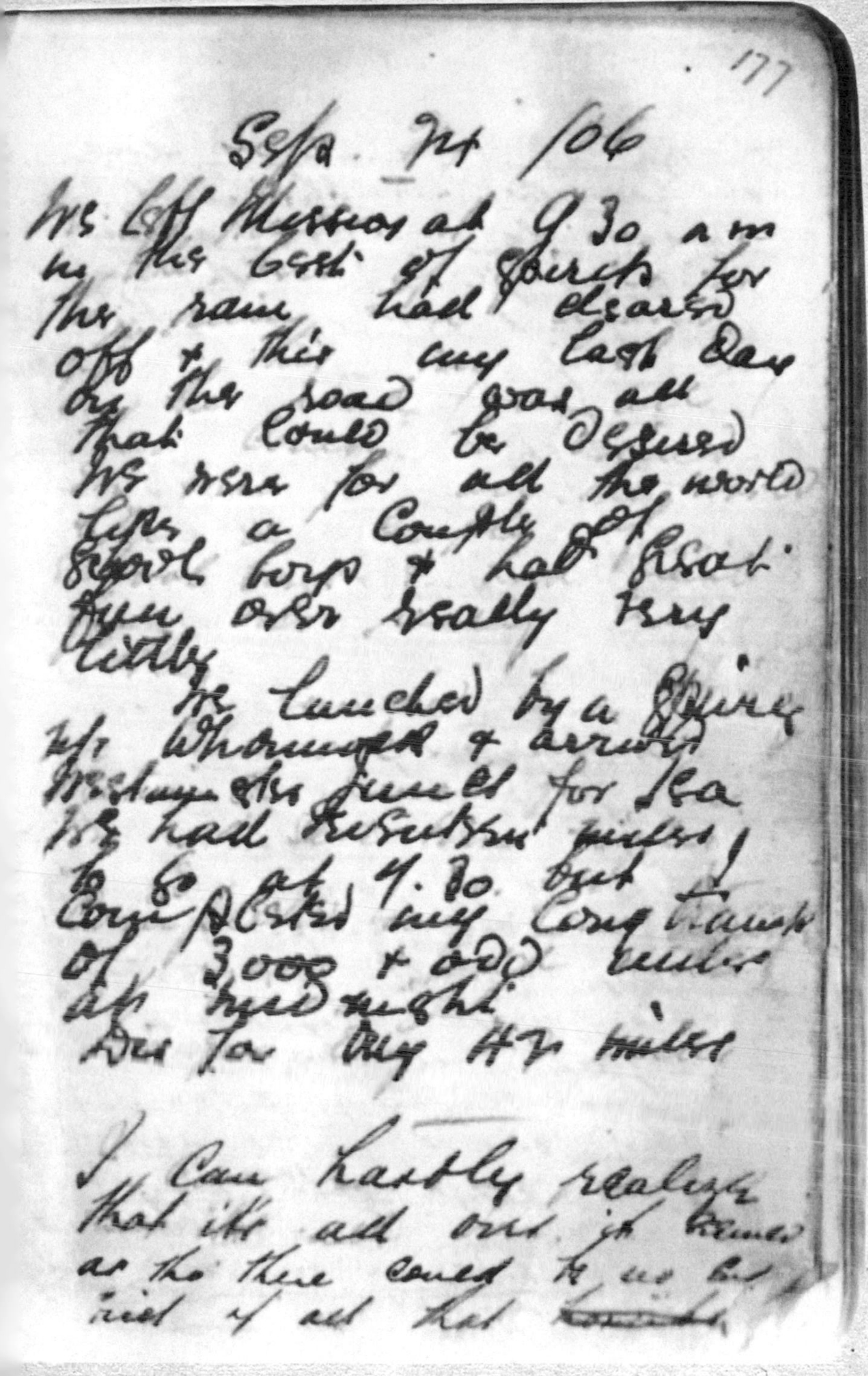

Sept. 9th /06

We left Wessos at 9.30 a.m.
in the best of spirits for
the rain had cleared
off + this my last day
on the road was all
that could be desired
We were for all the world
like a couple of
school boys + had Scot.
been over really very
little
We lunched by a ...
+ arrived
at ... for tea
We had Seventeen miles
to go at 4.30 but
Campbell my companion
of 3000 + odd miles
at midnight
Dist for day 47 miles

I can hardly realize
that it's all over. it seems
as tho there seemed to us but
... of all that ...

They registered at the Hotel Vancouver. John had two pieces of mail waiting for him. Don Parker wrote that the young eagle John had sent him had arrived safely. A letter from his father told him that his little sister Teresa, twelve years old, had died after a long illness. John remembered his gentle sibling with sadness.

Vancouver railway station

Tuesday morning at breakfast Gillis read an account on page 15 of *The Daily World* of how the Vancouver Athletic Club had defeated the Seattle Club 59 to 58 points in track and field at Brockton Point, winning the cup presented by that newspaper.[3] He could see that Vancouver took great interest in track and field.

But the big event on Tuesday was the arrival of the Governor General, Earl Grey, Lady Grey and the vice-regal party in Vancouver. All the ships in the harbour were decorated with bunting. About ten o'clock a.m. the *Quadra* steamed through the Narrows carrying the distinguished visitors. A guard of honour of militia and Boer War veterans, flanked by members of the fraternal societies, greeted them. Mayor Huscombe presented an illuminated address, to which His Excellency briefly replied. Then the parade began, marshalled by Captain Duff Stuart on horseback, followed by the carriages of dignitaries, and automobiles carrying prominent people, city councillors and Canadian Pacific Railway executives. Then came the Sixth Regimental Band; the militia and veterans; the Pipers Band in tartan, kilts and bonnets; the Sons of England in their blue sashes; the Orangemen in orange, blue and scarlet; the Mount Pleasant Band; Chiefs Joe Capillano and Charlie Cowichan leading their people in native dress; and, lastly, two brass bands. Cheered on by spectators the whole distance, the regal party wended its way to the Hotel Vancouver by circuitous route.

— • —

On Wednesday Gillis and Jackman were interviewed by a reporter of the *Daily News-Advertiser*, which carried a long article about the trek the next day. The *Victoria Daily Colonist* copied the piece word for word on Tuesday, October 2, 1906, on page three.

> Two powerful-looking young men each
> standing exactly six feet four and a half
> inches in height walked into Vancouver at

midnight on Monday, completing a long tramp across the continent from Sydney, N.S. It is perhaps the longest trip that has ever been undertaken in this manner in Canada. The pedestrians are J.H. Gillis of Sydney, N.S. and C.H. Jackman of Halifax, N.S.

Gillis left North Sydney intending to walk to Vancouver and return if possible within a year. This was to be done on a wager. However, being inexperienced with walking he found that it was a little more strenuous than he had anticipated and he will not be able to reach Sydney within the specified time. Mr. Jackman is a young Englishman of Halifax who travelled on foot for pleasure and the novelty of such a trip ... They will go down to Victoria for a few days and will return again about Sunday. Mr. Jackman will travel eastward in a railway coach while Gillis will again hit the high spots on his journey over the railway ties. Mr. Jackman started out from Montreal on April 16th ...

"Two other fellows started with me," said Gillis yesterday, "and it was our intention to go to San Francisco ... At Montreal my companions disagreed with me and I started westward alone. My companions got as far as Toronto and then went back home, where they arrived the latter part of May. When I was once under way I was bound I would stick it out. Many a time, though, during the first month I felt like dropping out. I had a terrible time with my feet and at first I could only make a few miles a day. This accounted for the slow time made during the trip. I also suffered considerably from the heat."

Both men spent the long weekend in Victoria, but by Wednesday, October 3, the time came for Charles to take the train to Toronto, where he would report to his company, before travelling on to Halifax. As the two trekkers walked down the platform for their goodbyes, they drew the usual attention. The men were rather quiet. Finally, Charles broke the silence.

"Never until now have two strangers become friends by tramping eighteen hundred miles together."

"Yes, and an Englishman and a Highlander at that. Like Roderick Dhu, I should have said to you when we met, 'Thy name and purpose, Saxon, stand.'"

Charles laughed, "Well, we crossed a lot of borders and never battled about one of them."

At the sonorous "ALL ABOARD" of the conductor, Charles gripped John's hand, "Cheerio, old chap, good luck and good health!"

"Tapadh Leibh, Thank you! Slainte Mhath Agus Sonas, Good health and happiness!"

They would never see each other again.

The Forgotten Champion

As John Hugh Gillis returned to Vancouver from the weekend in Victoria, he had a tough choice to make. Should he walk the railroad eastward, taking advantage of the offer of three pairs of walking boots gratis and seeking out friends made on the way westward, or should he stay in Vancouver, and seek ready employment. John Hugh wrote a letter to the *Sydney Daily Post* stating that he would set out soon on the return trip, but could not get back home until St. Patrick's Day 1907. He noted that "the trip across the prairies was a desperate one owing to the almost unbearable heat." The rainy season was just beginning in Vancouver and that weather would be intermittent for another month.

> It is not all sunshine making both ends meet out here. I have to depend on the sale of my post cards to pay expenses, and before a purchaser feels like

disgorging I have to make a spiel like a temperance exhorter.[1]

Eventually John Hugh decided to apply to join the Vancouver Police force. He wrote to Donald Parker to express regret that he had not been able to walk across the continent and back within a year and a day, and asked him to thank his associates for putting up the prize money. He told his brother-in-law that he had decided to stay in Vancouver because there was great interest and activity in track and field sports. While he awaited acceptance, Gillis took a job as a warehouseman and lived at 238 Barnard Street.[2]

By 1907 he was known as Jack Gillis of Vancouver track and field. He won the 120-yard hurdles in 19 seconds on August 14 of that year (and was ranked third nationally). At the same meet (in Vancouver), he placed first nationally in the high jump (5 feet 5 inches) and in the shot put (38 feet 6 inches).[3]

John Hugh also took a job as a clerk at the Pender Hotel[4] until he was inducted into the Vancouver Police on April 18, 1908, a fourth-class constable at a salary of $800, per annum.[5] The Force was attracted by his athletic prowess, and was well aware that he would bring renown to the Vancouver Police. John Hugh became a second physical director, working with athletic Duncan Gillis (no relation), formerly of Port Hood, Cape Breton, who had moved to Vancouver in 1900 at the age of nineteen and joined the police force.[6] The two men lived at 852 Cordova Street.[7]

Photo right: John (left) and Duncan Gillis

Transcontinental Pedestrians   239

John Gillis did not walk a beat. At a time when Vancouver had no police academy, his job was to help each recruit become as physically able as a law enforcement officer. His patience and determination set an example of the self-discipline and maximum effort required. Modest and unassuming, he helped new men build a sense of teamwork and pride. Apart from the regular push-up and sit-up exercises, frequent competitive events were the 220-yard run and the mile. John Hugh encouraged the more athletic recruits to develop their strengths.

In the Vancouver track-and-field meet on May 23, 1908 Jack Gillis was first in the 16-pound shotput (and at the Wanderers Stadium in Halifax on august 29, he came first nationally with a shotput of 40 feet 7 inches: it was a fine summer.[8]

The Winnipeg Tribune, Monday, July 19, 1909:

SENSATIONAL PERFORMANCES AT DOMINION CHAMPIONSHIPS

J.H. Gillis, Vancouver Policeman, Wins All-Round Championship

As was expected the Toronto team made a big cleanup but they were, nevertheless, given a great surprise by the two Vancouver policemen who toyed with the weights and jumps in a manner that had the Olympic stars beaten. D. Gillis took the hammer throw and the 56 lb. weight while J.H. Gillis secured the shot put, discus, high jump and hop, step and jump, besides a number of seconds and thirds. They will both make great men for the next Canadian Olympic team, and they are practically sure of places in the big events.

240

Winnipeg got a glimpse of the husky police-man, J.H. Gillis, from Vancouver, in the shot put. He was head and shoulder above all his competitors in this event, and won out in easy style.

D. Gillis showed class in the hammer throw, going 22 feet farther than his rival. J.H. Gillis took third in this event. [Duncan came first in the 56-pound weight at 32 feet 1 inch.]

J.H. Gillis, who won the hop-step-and-jump Saturday, is an old rival of Dr. McDonald, the Canadian champion at this event. The two Gillis boys are going to take in the police meets in the east. They should clean up in great style.

Manitoba Records Smashed (selected)

High Jump	J.H. Gillis, 6 ft. 1 inch
Discus –	J.H. Gillis, 112 ft. 9 inches; Duncan, 110 ft. 6 1/2 in
Hammer Throw –	D. Gillis, 145 ft. 2 inches
Shot Put –	J.H. Gillis, 43 ft. 2 inches[9]

John Hugh received letters of congratulation from his father, his brother Peter Dan, his sister Mary Jobe (the family historian), Don and Jessie Parker, his uncle Malcolm, and North Sydney friends. A letter from Charles Jackman pleased him and reminded him of a great and often trying adventure and a close friendship.

Globe newspaper clipping from July 28, 1909

In Toronto *The Globe* of July 28 featured a photograph of John H. Gillis, the "giant Vancouver policeman, who won the all-round championship of Canada at the C.A.A.U. annual championship meet at Winnipeg." The article noted that the Ottawa meet would be held at the Varsity Oval on July 29, and

J.H. Gillis, in full sporting regalia

would be marked by the "first" appearance of J.H. Gillis in Eastern Canada. The journalist did not know that both Gillis men were from the east and had cut their teeth in athletic events in Nova Scotia. In the competition both John and Duncan made a huge impression.

The Citizen, Ottawa, 29 July 1909:

GILLIS WON GOLD MEDAL

The two Gillis boys proved great attractions and soon became big favourites with the crowd, the splendid work of the British Columbia athletes evoking great enthusiasm. To John H. Gillis goes the gold medal for the all round championship. On the basis of three points for a first, two for a second and one for a third, John Gillis won no less than 21 points. He took first in the hop, step and jump, the 16 pound shot put, the 220 yards hurdles, throwing discus, and in the running long and the running high jumps. He was second in the standing broad jumps.

Gillis is tall and wiry, with long slim legs and a beautiful chest. He was graceful in every move despite his great height and in view of his gilt edged work at yesterday's meet it is no wonder that he landed the Canadian championship at Winnipeg. Duncan Gillis is also a strong acquisition to the field of Canadian amateur athletes. He was seen at his best in the heavyweight acts.

John H. Gillis had the misfortune while competing at Winnipeg two weeks ago to strain a muscle in his right knee. He also injured it at the beginning of yesterday's sports and was handicapped, on this account, in the running events, being forced to limp most of the afternoon. Gillis intends taking good care to see that nothing serious comes of the strain.[10]

Five thousand spectators crowded the Scarborough Beach Athletic Grounds to watch the Toronto Police twenty-seventh annual meet on Saturday, July 31, 1909. *The Globe* reported the following Monday that J.H. Gillis, the Western giant, won the gold medal with 20 points, placed first in five events, and came in second in two events, having placed in all events in which he competed. John Hugh was first in the running high jump, the 16-pound shot put, the running broad jump, the hop, step, and jump, and the 120-yard hurdles. He was second in the standing broad jump and in the discus throw.

John "Jack" Gillis in competition

D. Gillis, "his brother (sic) from the Vancouver force" won ten points with two firsts, one second and two thirds. Duncan was first in the discus throw and the 16-pound hammer throw, second in the 56-pound weight high throw and in the 16-pound shot put, and third in the 56-pound weight long throw.[11]

— • —

Four days later, Wednesday, August 4, at Britannia Park in Hamilton, the Gillis "cousins" of Vancouver scored only eleven points each, whereas the Hamilton force produced the first and second.

At Brockton Point Grounds in Vancouver on Saturday, September 18 of that year, the first annual championship meet

Brockton Point police games

of the British Columbia Amateur Athletic Union was held in cool weather with little wind. Jack Gillis, suffering from a weak back, unwisely engaged in the weight-throwing events. He did come first in the 16-pound shot, followed by Duncan, and second in the 120-yard hurdles and in the running high jump. Duncan Gillis, of the Vancouver Police Mutual Benefit Association, "toyed with the 56-pound weight and the discus."[12] If discus throwing had been on the program he would have received credit for breaking the North American record.[13]

Church Socials and Dancing

Inevitably there comes a time in a young man's life when he considers the possibility of settling down and having a family. John's friends had been suggesting he should think less about running, jumping and tossing and more about dancing and meeting girls. One night John relented and accompanied his pals to a church social at Holy Rosary Church on Richards Street. The sanctuary was only a few blocks from his apartment, and whenever he went to mass he could hear its eight bells ringing.

While dancing with a girl he knew, John noticed a young woman walking by on the arm of one of his friends. The woman noticed John's gaze and smiled. As John sat on the sidelines during the next dance, she introduced herself.

"Hello," John said, as he stood up. "I watched you on the dance floor."

"I noticed," she replied, looking up at him. "I've been reading about you in the papers."

The two danced, the tall, slim woman who stepped with

such vivacity and grace and the athletic giant with music in his feet. She was a natural blonde, with highlights in her hair. She had a rather large mouth and her eyes were an unusually brilliant blue. As John held her, he could feel great energy and yet gentleness. He was smitten. History has not left us her name, but the very next day, the pair went bicycling in Stanley Park. That summer they often went swimming at the beach.

Encouraged, John bought an engagement ring. The diamond was not very big but it was all he could afford, and one night with the moon on the water and the mountains shining in the distance, he proposed. They talked until late and decided that they would save up to get married after John returned from the Olympics and retired from track and field.

Heading for the 1912 Olympics

A strong track team from the Seattle Athletic Club took away the Vancouver Athletic Club's four-year championship, during the Brockton Point Meet on Saturday, July 29, 1910. The star was William Martin, the crack sprinter formerly of Notre Dame College. Jack Gillis won the all-round contest. The Vancouver competitors were divided between the Athletic Club and the Police Mutual Benefit Association, but their combined points did not match the performance of the visitors. Some criticized Jack Gillis because he had been a member of the VAC. At this meet, however, he competed under the colours of the Police Association because, in the all-round North American contest in Chicago two weeks away, he would be disqualified for representing two different organizations within a ninety-day period. Moreover, the Police Association had agreed to pay a large part of John's expenses to attend the Chicago meet. Duncan Gillis came first in throwing the 56-pound weight, the discus and the 16-pound hammer.[14]

The 1910 North American all-round championship was fought at Marshall Field, in Chicago, on Saturday, August 13, in a seesaw battle between F.C. Thomson of Los Angeles, the favourite, and J.H. Gillis. Their rivalry gripped the crowd of 3,500. The result was very close. Thomson scored 6,951 points and Gillis 6,909 – just 42 points short.[15] The winner of the third spot gained 6,120 points. The Amateur Athletic Union of the United States awarded Gillis the silver medal.[16] This was a

Gillis's competition medals

remarkable accomplishment for an athlete who had neither a trainer nor an advisor in attendance.

A crowd of 4,500 gathered at the Island Stadium for the Toronto Police athletic meet on Wednesday, August 17, 1910, when the threatening rain did not fall until the prizes were given out. John Hugh Gillis cleaned up with 21 points; his nearest competitor compiled 9. The sports reporter of *The Toronto Daily Star* wrote that Gillis did not look like an impressive athlete, being tall and spare. The crowd cheered when Constable Jack Dewis of Toronto defeated Gillis in the running broad jump.[18] *The Star* on the next page had a three-column photomontage of Gillis in action.[19]

The End of a Dream

On September 17, 1910, John Hugh Gillis suddenly resigned his position as first-class constable, and gave up his salary of twelve hundred dollars. The Vancouver Police Force had provided him with a useful profession, a good income, the opportunity to be an important member of its sports team, and leave and funds for travelling to various contests, sometimes distant. Why did he quit? His departure came exactly one month after the triumph at the Toronto Police Games and a month and four days after he had come close to winning the North American all-round gold medal. Feeling vaguely unwell, losing weight and always tired, John Hugh did not know what was wrong with him. The *Star* reporter had called him spare. He was.

This was a time of great personal crisis. His fiancée was much concerned about his health and his disappointment at his fading athletic strength. She came to see him often, sometimes with his best friend.

Announcing the world's all-round championship the next month, The Daily World mentioned "Vancouver's star athlete" and added, "Jack had intended to train early for this year's championship but later abandoned the intention."[20] He never did compete. John went to work for Customs, and lived at 347 Cordova Street.[21] He no longer had the energy to go out socially at night or on the weekend.

Finally, after a particularly miserable night, John Hugh wrote his fiancée a letter telling her he was in no condition to marry, and probably would not be for a long time. John was also afraid his illness was contagious, so he told her it was no longer safe to visit him. Besides, he suspected that his best friend was in love with her. Anyway, he told them they should stay away.

Gradually John Hugh grew worse; coughing, low fever, cold sweat at night, poor appetite, wasted appearance. On December 9, 1911, Dr. Kennedy admitted him[22] to the sanatorium at Tranquille, near Kamloops. Rate per week, $15. His closest relative was listed as A.H. Gillis, Glace Bay, N.S.

Galloping Consumption

The disease that crept up on John Hugh Gillis was tuberculosis, known then as "consumption" or "galloping consumption." For centuries this scourge caused distressing illness, and claimed many lives. European cities lost one in seven citizens to the "white plague." Four out of five North Americans became infected before age twenty, and five percent of those became ill within a year or two of infectious exposure. Early in the twentieth century, TB affected young and old and was the single most common cause of death.

> "More terrible than war, famine or pesti-lences ... [is] consumption, that annually sweeps away more of earth's inhabitants than any other disease known to the human race!" *The Montreal Star,* 15 March 1960[23]

People feared the illness and did not understand why it should strike some and not others. They tended to attribute a wrongness or shame to those affected. Often families would not mention that the disease had stricken a member. Even after German bacteriologist, Robert Koch discovered the bacillus responsible for tuberculosis in 1882 the myth continued that TB was a disease of the damp, foul air of crowded cities.

Patients were isolated in sanatoriums located in dry belts. There was no real cure for tuberculosis so, those institutions sought to provide good food, fresh air – frigid air on a balcony in winter and much bed rest.

Such was the regime that John Gillis entered at Tranquille, which was located a safe nine miles west of nervous Kamloops. Indeed, a few days after Gillis had first walked into Vancouver in 1906, Dr. Charles Fagan, the provincial health officer, was heading a strong appeal for funds all over the province for the erection of that first sanatorium in British Columbia.[24]

The Inland Sentinel welcomed John Gillis:[25]

JACK GILLIS VISITS KAMLOOPS

A well known and popular figure in the athletic world arrived here yesterday from the coast in the person of J.H. Gillis, holder of the all-round amateur championship of Canada. Gillis is a fine type of Canadian manhood, standing six feet four inches in height, and while at present he is not just up to his usual weight he expects the local climate and the training he enters into will soon have the effect of putting him into top class shape again. He intends to spend several months here and the training he will undertake is in preparation for entry in the all-round Olympic championship of the world in Stockholm next year. Gillis took second at the Chicago Olympic (sic) games last year and feels confident he can make even a better show. His last visit to Kamloops was in 1905 [really 1906] when he passed through on a walking tour from Sydney, N.S., to Vancouver, the undertaking being the result of a wager. He says he notes many changes, and in fact can scarcely believe the city of today has grown from the straggling village he remembers six years ago.

Tranquille's superintendent, Dr. Charles Vrooman, gave John a thorough physical examination upon arrival, and consigned him to bed for some time. When allowed to get up, John would rest on the balcony after his eight o'clock breakfast. His pulse, temperature and respiration were taken twice a day and recorded on his chart. He was prescribed light exercise, upon signs of improvement. This was slowly increased. In conversation with fellow patients, John did not discuss his illness nor did he encourage others to talk about theirs. Most men and women at the sanatorium were in the advanced stages of TB. John was not allowed to touch alcohol (which was thought to provoke tuberculosis), but he could smoke on the veranda or outside the buildings.[26] For entertainment he could read books and newspapers, write letters, do crafts or listen to music on a gramophone. His former fiancée wrote to him often and he wrote back with all the cheer at his command. Vancouver friends and Cape Breton family were far away. He said goodbye to the very few patients who returned home and to others who went out another door.

John suffered a spell of sadness and regret when the Fifth Olympic Games opened in Stockholm on May 5, 1912. He would have been there in the decathlon, going up against the great Native American athlete Jim Thorpe (whose gold medals were taken away because long ago he had received fifteen dollars for playing minor league baseball, and so could not be considered an amateur sportsman).

Duncan Gillis

After a time John became reconciled to not competing. His friends sent him newspapers so he could follow the Olympics right up to the closing day, on July 27. John Hugh was pleased that Canada won two gold medals: one in swimming and another in the 10,000-metre race walk. He cheered when he read that Duncan Gillis had won a silver medal tossing the weight.

Duncan Gillis had left the Vancouver Police and in 1911 joined with Vic Foley, a boxer, to found the Foley, Gillis & Company athletic club.[27] According to *The Toronto Star* of December 27, Duncan Gillis had become the all-round champion athlete of British Columbia. He was awarded two gold medals for weight tossing at the Pacific Coast championship track and field meet held at Astoria, Oregon, the summer before. At the Olympic games in Stockholm that year he won a silver medal for the 16-pound hammer throw, defeating the American athlete, Jim Thorpe. Later Duncan became Canada's wrestling champion. He was inducted in 1967 into the British Columbia Sports Hall of Fame as "one of the world's greatest all-around athletes," and into the Nova Scotia Sport Hall of Fame in 1999.

Decline

John Hugh Gillis was discharged from the Tranquille sanatorium on September 30, 1912. He moved to the Dominion Hotel in Kamloops.

The woman he had loved and almost married wrote to him to say she was engaged and would be marrying his friend in the spring. His friend had already written to tell him of their intentions.

Gillis bore himself with stoic dignity. He had made peace with himself, as gradually his body and health waned. Finally, he wrote his brother Peter Dan, with whom he had run so often as a boy, and his sister Jessie (Mrs. Donald Parker), asking them to come and take him home.

During the long days and nights of John Hugh's train trip from Kamloops to Cape Breton, he recognized the names of stations. He remembered the climb through the mountains with Jackman, the tunnels they rushed through, and the long bridges they raced across (in case of oncoming trains), the high, snowy peaks and long, deep canyons of the Rockies, the terrible, exhausting heat and often bad drinking water of the Prairies, the walk alone of a thousand miles from Montreal across Northern Ontario, the St. Patrick's Parade in Montreal, and the break-up with George and Jack. The snowstorms and frigid cold of Maine, and the generous people down east. All of which had happened only seven years earlier.

John Hugh settled in the home of his sister, Jessie Parker. She could not do enough for him. He did what he could with what strength he had left. John's father built a beautiful cabinet, which he placed in John's bedroom, and there, behind the glass doors, were arrayed the dozens of his medals. Quietly

JOHN HUGH GILLIS

Turn-of-the-century athlete died before he could attend Olympics

An Upper Margaree man whose athletic ability was Olympian in its potential, died before he could measure his ability against the best in the world.

John Hugh Gillis, born in Upper Margaree in 1884 to Angus

A nephew of Margaree Bard Malcolm H. Gillis, he walked from North Sydney to Vancouver. It took him three months. In Vancouver, he joined the police force and was a desk sergeant. His badge number was 23.

John Gillis's obituary from unnamed newspaper

and cheerfully, the champion with the big emaciated frame faded. Two weeks after his arrival in North Sydney, his breath and his heart failed. John Hugh Gillis died at Jessie's home, July 4, 1913. He was twenty-nine years old.

His obituaries were numerous, and unstinting in their praise of his career, character, and impact on Canadian sport. John Hugh Gillis was mourned all across the country.

— • —

In Oxford, Nova Scotia, Charles Jackman sat on a lawn chair in his garden and thought sadly about his young companion in their great adventure. He was sorry he had not kept in closer touch.

The Diarist

Before leaving on his long walk, Charles Jackman visited Nova Scotia where he met the woman with whom he fell in love. He had gone to Annapolis Royal to see his friend, Henry Bradford, the owner and headmaster of St. Andrew's School, a residential institute of such excellence that it attracted international students. Hearing "Liebestraum," he waited outside the door until it was finished. Then he wandered into the room and saw a

Charles Henry Jackman

Helen Fiske

beautiful young woman sitting at the piano.

She was a piano teacher at St. Andrews School in Annapolis Royal. Her name was Helen Fiske.

In 1906, when Charles returned from his long walk, he visited Helen Fiske. For Christmas, he gave her a leather-covered album of fifty-seven of the many snapshots he had taken on his walk. They became engaged and Charles, as an agent of a national flour milling company, began to save money to buy a house. The couple liked the little town of Oxford, Nova Scotia, for its beauty, and for its railway connections. They bought a large green house, on a corner lot.

On September 15, 1909, Charles Henry Jackman, 31, commercial traveller of Oxford, and Helen Hammond Fiske, 24, daughter of Amasa Homer Fiske, high school principal, and Eleanor Locke, were married at the Holy Cross Anglican Church in Lockeport. Their first child, Frances, was born the next summer and eighteen months later another daughter, Nan arrived. Soon after came Dorothy, Marion, Barbara Helen and Jean.

About two weeks after the birth of their fifth child, Charles went to Halifax to work on the relief committees coping with the devastation and the 9,000 injured and the 2,000 dead in the Halifax Explosion of December 6, 1917. Two square miles of rubble were on fire. A blizzard added to the suffering. He and many volunteers of the surrounding towns helped Haligonians bring the blind and wounded to medical relief, the homeless to find shelter, and the dead to take a place in the mortuary in Chebucto Road School. So painful were the memories of that experience that Charles never in his life spoke about them.

Intercolonial Railway Station, North Street,
after the Halifax explosion of 1917

Family Life

Charles was busy in Oxford. A charter member of the curling club, he took an active part in community affairs. He had an unused Anglican church hauled from the country to the town. A minister came off and on. Helen played the organ and Charles took up the collection. As their seven children grew old enough, all sang in the choir. Charles owned a park, which he opened to the public. He also began operating a gravel pit on the side to earn a little money from the road builders. The Jackman girls drove their horse and sleigh in winter, and in a special cart in summer. Bess, the Shetland Island pony, patiently hauled the youngest ones. Every morning, after his cold shower, Charles would knock on bedroom doors, enter, raise all windows to the top, even in winter with the snow blowing in, and announce cheerily, "Rise and shine, it's a beautiful day."

This was a happy time for all the Jackmans.

Pictou

After twenty-one years in land-locked Oxford, the Jackmans moved to Pictou.

Charles found a large house on a hill on the corner of Denoon and Palmerston Streets. From the top front windows, the family had a magnificent view of the harbour. Built by a sea captain, the big gabled structure had high ceilings, inside shutters for tall windows and, in addition to radiators, a fire-place in every room including the spacious bathroom, which was panelled in solid mahogany. Elm and oak trees sheltered the terraced lawn.

The Jackman home in Pictou, Nova Scotia

Finances sometimes got a bit tight as the result of Charles's generosity and the expense of Helen's succession of hearing aids and the hospitalization of their two daughters. Charles would cheerfully don his best suit, put a red rose in his lapel and go down to see the banker. "No use being poor and looking poor," he would say. Off he would stride with his habitual cane.

Charles became a town councillor and president of the school board in his retirement. His contribution to the war effort and to his reduced income was to serve as a night watchman at the Pictou shipyards. He reread some of the books, like *The Pickwick Papers*, that he had enjoyed years ago. Occasionally he recounted to service clubs or schools the adventures of the long walk with his friend Gillis. He was amused at a persistent story in the town that Mr. Jackman had walked across Canada to advertise Dexter boots and shoes and that the company had awarded him free shoes for the rest of his life. As it was, he had to pay for special shoes to fit his outsized feet.

Charles continued to walk. At the age of seventy-five he turned up one day at the family summer cottage, twelve miles from Pictou, announcing, "I've brought your mail."

Helen had a stroke at the age of sixty-nine and spent seven years in a Halifax nursing home. Charles lived on in the Pictou house for three years, lonely and missing his wife. His eldest daughters moved him to Halifax where he died, in his eightieth year, on March 9, 1958. Helen Hammond Pioke died three years later to the day, March 9, 1961.

Left: Helen and Charles Jackman in their garden

What Happened to George and John McDonald

THE SECOND AND THIRD WALKERS

George Cumming

George Cumming moved to Montreal where, on April 27, 1910, he married. From 1915 until invalided out toward the end of the First World War, he served in France with the 77th Battalion. He was forty-one years old when he signed up to serve overseas but he guaranteed his acceptance by deducting two years from his age. He was recorded as a chef, five feet four inches in height, living at 366 First Avenue, Verdun. From Flanders to the Somme he kept in a pocket a postcard bearing the photographs of his wife and two daughters, his entire family of the time. His discharge papers show that he had been gassed and that he had shrapnel in an arm. These fragments caused infection but although some were removed in hospital, nine finally remained.

In 1921 George brought his family to New Glasgow with him when he became head chef of the Norfolk Hotel. After six years the condition of George's arm worsened. He and his wife and their three boys and three girls later moved back to Montreal. George worked at a railway crossing, where he saved a boy in a close call from a train and was so upset that he could not stay on the job.

George was a generous man. One day he brought home a man and told Gertrude that Mr. McLean would be staying with them until he got on his feet. The man chopped wood, helped out, ate with the family and stayed the winter. Another time, as the weather was growing colder, he noticed a woman sitting on a bench for hours, each day he passed by on a stroll. When he asked why, she told him she was living with her daughter-in-law and had to leave the house each day so that she could have the place to herself. He went to City Hall and got her on welfare and found a small apartment for her. She later made the desserts for his daughter Ida's wedding reception.

George Walker Cumming died December 18, 1940, at the age of sixty-six and was buried in Côte-des-Neiges Cemetery in the Quillan family plot.[1] At his death his three sons were serving in the Second World War, two in the army and one in the navy.[2] His wife, Gertrude, lived twenty-four years more in their family home.[3] When she died and the house was cleared, two small black boxes that contained George's news clippings and other mementos of his long walk were thrown out.[4,5]

The *Eastern Chronicle* of December 24, 1940,[6] carried this obituary:

George Walker Cumming

Word comes from Montreal telling of the death there of George Walker Cumming, who was so well known in New Glasgow, the place of his birth, and in Cape Breton, where he lived for a time. He was a veteran of the Great War and a unique character in many ways. He will best be remembered by the name of "Punk" and with his wit he was like a flash of sunshine in any company. We have no recollection of ever hearing of George having any enemies, quite the contrary[;] few had so many friends, nor do we ever recollect of him being in bad humor. He could interject a stream of good nature into any company and his "come back" to a sally was quick and often extremely clever. Last year he visited the old home town for a few weeks, the guest of his sister Mrs. George Gammon, Abercrombie Road, and found many changes. Mr John Cumming is a brother and also Reuben Cumming of Boston. George is married and leaves a wife and large family in Montreal. They will have the deepest Sympathy of the friends of the family in New Glasgow.

John McDonald

In spite of advertisements offering a reward for information, and search of vital documents and military records, we have not found any trace of John McDonald or his family after his return from the long walk. The search continues.

Notes

CHAPTER ONE

1   Powers, Stephen. *Afoot and Alone* 2nd ed. New York: Columbian Book Company, 1884.

2   Lummis, Charles. *A Tramp Across the Continent*. New York: Charles Scribners Sons, 1903.

3   "Will Walk to San Francisco." *Sydney Daily Post* 29 Jan. 1906, front page.

4   "Pedestrians Left on Long Trip," *op.cit.* 1 Feb, 1906, sports page.

5   *1901 Census of North Sydney, page 5, family 126.*

6   "Will Walk to San Francisco." *Sydney Daily Post* 29 Jan. 1906, front page.

7   Macdonald, Clyde F. *More Notable Pictonians*. Pictou: author, 2004, pages 30-47

8   The Attestation Papers of George W. Cumming, 8 Aug 1915, recorded his height as 5 feet 4 inches.

9   "Will Walk to San Francisco." *Sydney Daily Post* 29 Jan 1906, front page.

10   "Walking to 'Frisco." *The Sydney Record* 1 Feb. 1906, page 5.

11   1901 Census of Pictou.

12   Pictou County Birth Registrations, numbers 668, 669.

13   *1901 Transcribed Census of Pictou Town*. Pictou County

Genealogical and Heritage Society.

14   Cape Breton County Marriage registrations, page 167, entry 295.

15   "Transcontinental Travellers in Moncton." *The Daily Times* 21 Feb. 1906, page 5.

16   "Walking to 'Frisco'." *The Sydney Record* 1 Feb. 1906, page 5.

17   "Obituary." *The Sydney Record* 15 Mar. 1955, page 3.

CHAPTER TWO

1   "Walking to 'Frisco'." *The Sydney Record* 1 Feb. 1906, page 5.

2   "Cummings Set Out After Gillis." *Sydney Daily Post* 2 Feb. 1906, front page.

3   *Ibid.*

4   Gillis, Margaret E. "From Morar to Margaree." *West Word* July 2004, pages 11-13.

5   "The Long Distance Walk." *Sydney Daily Post* 2 Feb. 1906, page 3.

6   *Ibid.*

7   "McDonald Wouldn't Return." *Sydney Daily Post* 3 Feb. 1906, page 3.

8   "Three Young Men from North Sydney." *Antigonish Casket* 8 Feb. 1906, page 8.

9   Letter from Kathleen MacKinnon, Archivist 19 May 2004.

10   "Indoor Meet." *The Excelsior* Dec. 1902, page 110.

11   "For a Purse of $600." *Pictou Advocate* 6 Feb. i906, front page.

12   "Pedestrians Now at New Glasgow." *The Sydney Record* 9 Feb, 1906, front page.

13   "Well Along the Road." *Sydney Daily Post* 10 Feb 1906, page 3.

14   "The Transcontinental Pedestrians." *Eastern Chronicle* 13 Feb. 1906, front page.

15   "Ocean to Ocean Men Heard From." *Sydney Daily Post* 13 Feb., page 3.

16   "Afoot Across the Continent." *Truro Daily News* 12 Feb. 1906, page 5.

17   "A Friend at Glengarry." *Pictou Advocate* 27 Feb. 1906, front page.

18   "That Glengarry Affair." *Amherst News* 26 Feb. 1906; *The Sydney Daily Post* 1 Mar. 1906, page 2.

19   "Reached Amherst." *Sydney Daily Post* 19 Feb. 1906, page 5.

20   "Afoot Across the Continent" *Truro Daily News* 12 Feb. 1906, page 5.

21   "Probably They Did Right." *Truro Daily News* 22 Feb. 1906, page 6.

CHAPTER THREE

1   "Transcontinental Travellers in Moncton." *The Daily Times* 19 Feb. 1906, page 3.
2   "Transcontinental Trotters Pass Through Moncton." *The Moncton Transcript* 19 Feb. 1906, front page.
3   "Made Fuss Over Pedestrians." *The Sydney Record* 24 Feb. 1906, page 8.
4   "Are They Walking?" *Saint John Globe*, 22 Feb. 1906, page 3; *The Moncton Transcript* 23 feb. 1906, page 2; *The Sydney Record* 1 Mar. 1906, page 8.
5   "Will Go to 'Frisco If Roads are Good." *Evening Times* 21 Feb. 1906, front page.
6   "Started Again." *Saint John Globe*, 24 Feb. 1906, page 5.
7   "Expect to Be in Montreal." *Sydney Daily Post* 3 Mar. 1906, page 2.
8   "Note from the Pedestrians." *op.cit.* 5 Mar. 1906, page 2.
9   "Exciting Times on Walking Tour." *London Free Press* 6 Apr. 1906, page 3.
10   *Ibid*
11   "Travellers Heard From." *Sydney Daily Post* 8 March 1906, page 5.
12   "Ocean to Ocean Men." *op. cit.* 14 Mar. 1906, page 3.
14   "Are Tramping to San Francisco." *Sherbrooke Daily* 10 Mar. 1906, front page.
14   "No. Sydney Boys in Montreal." *Sydney Daily Post* 17 Mar. 1906, page 2.

CHAPTER FOUR

1   Mark Gendron, of Seattle, physical trainer and former Olympic athlete, provided useful information about the practical treatment of plantar fascitis.
2   "No. Sydney Boys in Montreal." *Sydney Daily Post* 17 Mar. 1906, page 2.
0   Useful for addresses and other information was *Lovell's Montreal Directory for 1906-1907*. Montreal: John Lovell & Sons, 1907.
4   "Wanderers Win Stanley Cup." *Montreal Star* 19 Mar. 1900.
5   "Pontifical Mass at St. Patrick's." *op.cit*
6   "St. Patrick's Parade." *op.cit.*

CHAPTER FIVE

1   "On a Wager." *Ottawa Citizen* 27 Mar. 1906, front page.
2   "Pedestrians Parted." *Sydney Daily Post* 24 Mar. 1906, front page.
3   "Cummings and McDonald Took Cold Feet." *The Sydney Record* 31

Mar. 1906, page 8.

4   "Cummings and McDonald Are Still Walking." *The Sydney Record* 24 Mar. 1906, page 8.

5   "Transcontinental Tourists." *The Daily Intelligencer* 26 Mar. 1906, page 7.

6   "Exciting Times on Walking Tour." *London Free Press* 6 Apr. 1906, page 3.

7   "Eaton's Daily Store News." *The Toronto Daily Star* 28 Mar. 1906.

8   Advertisements. *The Globe* 28 Mar. 1906.

9   "Pedestrians Heard From." *Sydney Daily Post* 5 Apr. 1906, page 2.

10   "Exciting Times on Walking Tour." *London Free Press* 6 Apr. 1906, page 3.

CHAPTER SIX

1   1901 Census of Harrogate, Yorkshire, RG13, Piece 4052, Folio 50, Page 31, Schedule 190, household of Fanny Jackman, 12 West End Avenue.

2   "Lacrosse North of England Championship Competition." *The Advertiser* (Stockport, Manchester, England) 28 Oct. 1898, page 2.

3   "Lacrosse North V. England." *The Advertiser* 17 Sept 1897, page 2; "Lacrosse North V. South." *The Advertiser* 14 April 1899, page 2.

4   "Comment on Current Sporting Topics." *The Globe* 3 July 1903, page 10.

5   "Mr. Cawthra's Team Won." *The Globe* 3 July 1903, page 10.

6   "Halifax to San Francisco." *Kalamazoo Semi-Weekly Telegraph* 24 Apr. 1906, page 3.

7   "Two Young Pedestrians Crossing the Continent." *The Morning Enquirer* (Battle Creek) 19 Apr. 1906.

8   "Lacrosse North V. South." *The Advertiser* 14 April 1899, page 2.

CHAPTER SEVEN

1   "Two Peculiar Visitors Arrive in the City." *The Daily Standard* (St. Catharines) 2 May 1906.

2   "Had Only 10 Cents." *Sydney Daily Post* 4 May 1906.

3   "St. Joseph's Lone Pedestrian." *Sydney Daily Post* 2 May 1906, page 2.

4   "Transcontinental Traveler en Route." *Daily Times Journal* (Fort William) 6 May 1906; page 3.

5   "Walking Across the Continent, Charles Jackman Reaches North Bay." *The Toronto Daily Star* 4 May 1906, page 14.

6   "Tramped Across the Continent: Two Wager Seekers Arrive in Toronto." *The Toronto Daily Star* 5 May 1906, front page.
7   "Slightly Inaccurate." *Sydney Daily Post* 9 May 1906, front page.
8   "Pedestrians Faking." *Sydney Daily Post* 11 May 1906, page 5.

CHAPTER EIGHT

1   "A Letter from Gillis." *Sydney Daily Post* 29 May 1906, page 2.
2   "Ogilvie Elevator a Complete Wreck." *Daily Times Journal* (Fort William) 28 May 1906, front page.
3   "Walking Across Canada, C.H. Jackman at Port Arthur." *The Toronto Daily Star* 30 May 1906, page 10.
4   "Those Fast Walkers Making a Record." *The Montreal Star* 2 June 1906, front page.
5   "A Pipe Dream." *Sydney Daily Post* 29 May 1906, page 2.
6   "Another Pipe Dream." *Sydney Daily Post* 1 June 1906, page 2.

CHAPTER NINE

1   "Still Stringing Them." *Sydney Daily Post* 8 June 1906, page 5.
2   "Letter from J.H. Gillis." *Sydney Daily Post* 26 June 1906, page 2.
3   "Pedestrian Home." *Sydney Daily Post* 27 June 1906, page 2.
4   "Gillis Is Still Plodding Along." *Sydney Daily Post* 11 July 1906, page 4.
5   "A Pedestrian Home. *Sydney Daily Post* 10 July 1906, page 5.
6   "George Cumming Crossed Atlantic." *Sydney Record* 14 July 1906, front page.

CHAPTER TEN

1   "Walking from Ocean to Ocean." *The Daily Standard* (Regina) 20 July 1906, pages 1 and 4.
2   "J.H. Gillis Transcontinental Pedestrian." *The Leader Post* (Regina) 20 July 1906.

CHAPTER ELEVEN

1   "Transcontinental Tramps." *Revelstoke Mail Herald* 8 Sept 1906,
2   Working in the prison brickyard, Bill Miner, over time, dug a hole away from the guard's night. Then one night with three others he crept to the outer wall, picked the lock on a toolshed, and with a ladder climbed over the wall. Some said that the Canadian Pacific Railway engineered his escape in return for the cached bonds worth 50,000 pounds. With the spoils from a train robbery in Oregon he enjoyed a long vacation in Europe. In February of 1911

he and two others held up the Southern Express in Georgia, for which he was soon arrested, tried and sentenced to twenty years. Escaping six months later, he was captured and put in chains. He sawed through his chains and window bars and escaped but a day in a horrible swamp led to the prison hospital and his death at the age of sixty-six. Considering Bill Miner to have qualities not found in the average convict, the Sunday School teacher saved his body from being sent to a medical school, bought a casket and burial plot and arranged an Episcopal service, at which many attended. With his intelligence, charm, daring and ingenuity, William McDonald, alias Miner, might have had a distinguished career on the other side of the law. A thorough book on the subject is: Anderson, Frank W. *Bill Miner: Stagecoach and Train Robber.* Surrey, B.C.: Heritage House, 1983.

3   "Vancouver Holds the World's Cup." *The Daily World* 24 Sept. 1906. page 3.

4   "Our Guest." *The Daily News-Advertiser* 26 Sept. 1906, page 7.

CHAPTER TWELVE

1   "The North Sydney Athlete On His Way Back from Pacific." *Sydney Daily Post* 6 Oct.1906, front page.

2   *Henderson's City of Vancouver Directory.* Vancouver, BC: Henderson Publishing Company, 1907.

3   Radcliffe, Ted and McNulty, William. *Canadian Athletics 1839-1992.* Ottawa: Athletics Canada, 1992.

4   *Henderson's City of Vancouver Directory.* Vancouver, BC: Henderson Publishing Company, 1908.

5   Information received from Barbara Fenwick, Archivist, Vancouver Police Museum.

6   BC Sports Hall of Fame. "Highlights, Duncan Gillis, inducted 1967.

7   *Henderson's City of Vancouver Directory.* Vancouver, BC: Henderson Publishing Company, 1909 and 1910.

8   Radcliff & McNulty. *op. cit.*, page 20.

9   "Sensational Performance at Dominion Championships." *Winnipeg Tribune* 19 July 1909, page 6.

10   "Gillis Won Gold Medal." *The Ottawa Citizen* 29 July 1909, page 8.

11   "The Police Athletics." *Toronto Globe*, 2 Aug. 1909, page 3.

12   "Gillis Cousins Third at Hamilton." *Toronto Star* 5 Aug. 1909, page 10.

13   "Record Breaking Track Meet at Brocton Point." *The Daily Province* 20 Sept. 1909, page 3.

14   "P.N.A. Meet Is Won by Seattle's Team." *The World* 1 Aug. 1910, sports page.

15   "Vancouver Cop Always in the Hunt." *Toronto Star* 15 Aug. 1910, page 11.

16   "Gillis Good Second in All-Round Contest." *The Daily World* 15 Aug. 1910, sports page.

17   "Jack Gillis Earned Distinction for Vancouver in Last Year's Contests." *The Daily World* 5 Aug. 1911, sports page.

18   "Gillis Champion of Local Police." *The Toronto Daily Star* 18 Aug. 1910, page 12.

19   "J.H. Gillis, the Vancouver Policeman." *The Toronto Daily Star* 18 Aug. 1910, page 13.

20   "World's All Round Championship This Month." *The Daily World* 5 Aug. 1911, sports page.

21   *Henderson's City of Vancouver Directory.* Vancouver: Henderson Publishing Company, 1911.

22   *Admission Book, Anti-Tuberculosis Society Records 1907-1947.* British Columbia Archives, MS-1916, vol. 7.

23   "Advertisement." *The Montreal Star* 15 Mar. 1906, page 13.

24   "Appeal for Funds." *Daily News-Advertiser* 6 Oct. 1906.

25   "Jack Gillis Visits Kamloops." *The Inland Sentinel* 8 Dec. 1911.

26   Norton, Wayne. *A Whole City by Itself: Tranquille and Tuberculosis.* Kamloops: Plateau Press, 1999.

27   "Sports Note." *The Toronto Star* 27 Dec. 1911, page 13.

CHAPTER FOURTEEN

1   Macdonald, Clyde F. *More Notable Pictonians.* Pictou: Advocate Publishing, 2004, pages 30-33.

2   Attestation Paper, Canadian Overseas Expeditionary Force, No. 144680, Folio 21.

3   Letter and Notes, 3 March 2005, from George Cumming's granddaughter July Maliff to the author.

4   *Ibid*

5   *Ibid*

6   Obituary, *Eastern Chronicle*, 24 December 1940, page 8.

Photo Credits

Page 23 Library and Archives Canada, PA-061883; page 26 photo taken by Charles Jackman, courtesy of the author; page 28 courtesy of the author; page 32 photo by P.N. Crandell, Moncton, 1906, courtesy of Beaton Institute, Cape Breton University, no. 83-661-13962; page 54 Queen's Square, Saint John, ca. 1906 © 1999-2005 Department of Supply and Services Provincial Archives of New Brunswick; page 60 CPR Station Hotel – McAdam, courtesy of McAdam Historical Restoration Commission; page 61 Fire at I.R.C. Shops – Moncton, NB, February 24th 1906, © 1999-2005 Department of Supply and Services Provincial Archives of New Brunswick; page 07 top: © Deborah M. Fowles, bottom. photo by Larry Goss; page 73 photo taken by Charles Jackman, courtesy of the author; page 79 Courtesy of the McCord Museum, MP-1798.207.1.22; page 86 Gillis Souvenir card, 1906, courtesy of Beaton Institute, Cape Breton University no. 83-661-13961; page 87 Le Grand Magasin de W.H. Scroggie, Limited 1905, courtesy of the Bibliothèque et Archives Nationales Quebec; page 88 photo taken by Charles Jackman, courtesy of the author; page 90 the Montreal Wanderers, Library and Archives Canada, public domain; page 92 courtesy of D. Stiebeling, photographer; page 100 courtesy of the City of Toronto Archives, Series 330, File 12; page 101 courtesy of the City of Toronto Archives, Fonds 1244, Item 2; page 117 photo taken by Charles Jackman, courtesy of the author; page 126 photo taken by Charles Jackman, courtesy of the author; page 140-141 courtesy of the author; page 143 top and bottom photos taken by Charles Jackman, courtesy of the author; page 148 photo taken by Charles Jackman, courtesy of the author; page 156 photo taken by Charles Jackman, courtesy of the author; page 157 courtesy of the author; page 159 photo taken by Charles Jackman, courtesy of the author; page 160 photo taken by Charles Jackman, courtesy of the author; page 161 photo taken by Charles Jackman, courtesy of the author; page 162 photo taken by Charles Jackman, courtesy of the author; page 164 from Winnipeg Illustrated, 1911 public domain; page 168 photo taken by Charles Jackman, courtesy of the author; page 170 photo taken by Charles Jackman, courtesy of the author; page 176 photo taken by Charles Jackman, courtesy of the author; page 177 photo taken by Charles Jackman, courtesy of the author; page 186 courtesy of the author; page 193 photo taken by Charles Jackman, courtesy of the author; page 195 photo taken by Charles Jackman, courtesy of the author; page 201 photo taken by Charles Jackman, courtesy of the author; page 202 photo taken by Charles Jackman, courtesy of the author; page 204 top and bottom photos taken by Charles Jackman, courtesy of the author; page 206 top and bottom photos taken by Charles Jackman, courtesy of the author; page 208 photo taken by Charles Jackman, courtesy of the author; page 213 photo taken by Charles Jackman, courtesy of the author; page 217 photo courtesy of R.C.M.P. Archives, Ottawa; page 218 courtesy of Fred Thirkell and Bob Scullion, *British Columbia 100 Years Ago: Portraits of a Province*, Surrey, B.C.: Heritage House Publishing Co. Ltd., 2002; page 224 courtesy of B.C. Archives photo# A-04669; page 225 courtesy of B.C. Archives photo# I-22437; page 227 courtesy of the author; page 228 courtesy of Fred Thirkell and Bob Scullion, *British Columbia 100 Years Ago: Portraits of a Province*, Surrey, B.C.: Heritage House Publishing Co. Ltd., 2002; page 230-231 courtesy of the author; page 232 courtesy of Fred Thirkell and Bob Scullion, British Columbia 100 Years Ago: Portraits of a Province, Surrey, B.C.: Heritage House Publishing Co. Ltd., 2002; page 239 courtesy of the author; page 242 courtesy of the author; page 243 from *The Globe* 28 July, 1909, p. 9; page 245 City of Vancouver Archives; page 246 courtesy of the author; page 249 courtesy of the author; page 259 courtesy of the author; page 260 courtesy of the author; page 261 photo taken by Charles Jackman, courtesy of the author; page 263 courtesy of the author; page 264 courtesy of the author.